T0164651

Where's My Sister?

My Little Sister's Struggle with Addiction, Adoption, and Mental Illness

Linda Burden

iUniverse, Inc.
Bloomington

Where's My Sister?
My Little Sister's Struggle with Addiction,
Adoption, and Mental Illness

iUniverse books may be ordered through booksellers or by contacting:

iUniverse
1663 Liberty Drive
Bloomington, IN 47403
www.iuniverse.com
1-800-Authors (1-800-288-4677)

ISBN: 978-1-4620-0381-5 (sc)
ISBN: 978-1-4620-0382-2 (dj)
ISBN: 978-1-4620-0383-9 (ebk)

Library of Congress Control Number: 2011903800

Printed in the United States of America

iUniverse rev. date: 4/5/2011

Acknowledgments

For my friends who read, and encouraged the writing of this book: Katherine, Donna, Jennifer, Laure, Pam. Thanks to Alison and Mike for always being there and LeAnn and Michelle for their loving friendship and care of my sister and my daughter, Vida, for her editing suggestions, and to my son, Pablo, for all those great healthy meals and to K for working so hard to make Alley's trip to Greece memorable.

For Alison:

Here is your book.

Contents

Introduction

Alison arrived in the summer before I started first grade. I remember the day my parents brought her home. My grandmother was staying with me, my brother was away at overnight camp, and Mother and Dad had gone to get the new baby.

I remember the day because I was five years old—a big girl. My mother and father walked in the house, with my mother carrying the baby wrapped up in a blanket. My grandmother sat down in a chair in the dining room, and Mother put the bundle in her arms. My mother called me to come inside.

"Come over and say hi to your new baby sister," she said.

I looked down at hair so yellow I could see through it. Her big brown eyes looked up at me. It was not love at first sight. When you are five, a baby isn't all that much fun.

We grew up in a little town in Vermont's Champlain Valley. We lived on an elm- and chestnut-lined road—the kind of road where your mother knew everything you had done that day before you walked in the door. Our house sat between two dairy farms. In the summer, I remember falling asleep to the hum of the giant fans cooling the haylofts.

We were the perfect family: two parents, a son, a daughter, and now a second daughter. We were "lucky kids"; everyone said so. We had been adopted into a good family and lived in a nice colonial house my parents had built. In front, inside a circular driveway, grew a huge evergreen my father strung with Christmas lights the day after Thanksgiving. Two cars sat in the garage, a basketball hoop hung above the overhead doors, and a black Lab ran around the yard.

My best friends lived within walking distance; together, we rode bikes and horses and hiked up the hill in the summer, and we sled down the hill in the winter.

My mother and father were tall and good-looking. My father had a good job, and my mother was a full-time mother. Their first child was a handsome son and a talented athlete. I, their second child and first daughter, was cute, if I do say so myself, with dark eyes and hair. And now they had a new baby.

My parents had many friends in town, and get-togethers for dinner and drinks were common. Every house had an open bar, and when someone came to visit, the first line was, "What will you have?"

Our world was like a greeting card. It looked perfect.

But it wasn't perfect. Mother and Dad had not dealt with the deaths of their two biological children. They adopted my older brother, Bob, and me to replace their dead son and daughter. The little girl had died at four and a half in surgery and the little boy before he was a year old.

Mother, at eighteen, had unknowingly married an alcoholic. She would call him in sick, lie for him when he drove his car into a ditch would pretend everything was fine as they borrowed money from family and friends. Shortly after Alison was adopted, Dad lost his good job and Mother met an older man who told her she was beautiful. Not working gave Dad more time to drink. He would get up before dawn to get an early start and then fall back asleep by noon. This gave Mother an excuse to leave and to spend time with the man who, years later, would become her second husband. Her leaving gave Dad more time and an additional justification to drink.

Bob and I were eight and six, and Alison was only one year old.

Chapter One: Day One

I look at my watch to see if we are going to land on time. It has taken me all day to travel from Burlington, Vermont, to St. George, Utah, with three flight changes. The last leg of this is a short commuter flight on SkyWest from LAX to SGU. Each time I have flown out here to visit Alison, the landscape has never failed to amaze me. The bumpy flight over the Mojave Desert, the Sierra Nevada Mountains, Death Valley, and the Shoshone Mountains has me tightening my seat belt, and I remind myself these planes make this trip several times a day, and the wings are still attached. The thought doesn't comfort me much each time the planes hits a downdraft and the plane bounces. Finally, we land.

Clearing the door, I walk down the exterior stairs to the tarmac. The hot, dry desert air and high altitude take my breath away. I had told Alley on the phone I would be arriving at 4:40 p.m. My giving her the exact time gave her certainty that I was returning. I hurry through the terminal, carrying just my backpack, and into the parking lot, I look up and down the rows of cars for my sister's white Subaru Forester. I find it. The key is in the wheel well with the spare tire, and a piece of notebook paper left on the driver's seat offers directions to the hospital.

"Where's my sister?" The familiar voice greets me as the elevator doors retreat into the walls, replacing my reflection in the shiny surface with a larger-than-life watercolor of oversized flowers stuffed into southwestern clay pots mounted on the wall, welcoming me to the third floor.

"Where's my sister?" Her voice sounds as if she has been screaming at a Red Sox game that has gone into extra innings. "Where's my sister?" Her tone is insistent and demanding.

Once, Alley had been outgoing and fun, buying drinks for everyone, but now, her life consists of sitting all alone in her house, watching television with a cigarette in one hand and a drink in the other.

"Where's my sister?" she calls out again. A part of her brain has forgotten how to behave in public. She can no longer read the environment she is in and behave appropriately, and even if she could, I don't think she would bother.

"Where's my sister?' she demands. I hope she has not been screaming all day. I think of the other patients and staff having to endure the inescapable rudeness she has up to this point reserved just for me and her partners. I turn left at the corner of the hallway and break into a slow jog.

"Where's my sister? Where's my sister?" her strained hoarse voice says over and over. It is her mantra. She is like a stuck recording; I will reset it with my presence in order to keep this refrain from repeating over and over until she runs out of energy. "Where's my sister?"

A nurse dressed in colorful scrubs walks down the hall toward me. I feel heat rush to my face with embarrassment, as if a bubble over my head says, "I'm the sister, and I am responsible."

"Are you the sister?"

"Yep, I'm the sister." She reacts with a slight turning up of the corners of her mouth and a nod that suggests humor or relief, but not irritation, as she passes by.

Alison loves to entertain and has a talent for being the center of attention. Inconspicuousness is not one of her qualities.

"Where's my sister? Where's my sister?" she chants. I wonder how long this has been going on. I certainly don't need to stop at the nurse's station to ask for Alley's room number. I follow the voice down the hall.

"Are you the sister?"

I slow my pace and look at the nurse standing behind the half wall surrounding the nurse's work area.

"Yes, I'm the sister," I confess again. I see the nurse's face soften with relief. I know that look. It is the relief I always saw on the faces of bartenders when I fetched my drunken father from local bars.

The nurse nods as her eyes move from my face to someone over my left shoulder. I turn and see a woman who looks very much in charge.

"You must be the sister," she states rather than asks. She is standing next to the door, just out of view of her patient.

"Yes, I'm Linda." I feel as if I am in a sequel. Instead of rescuing my alcoholic father years ago I am now rescuing my alcoholic sister.

"We need to talk," says the nurse, taking a half step back, indicating I should move away from the door.

"I—" I begin.

"Where's my sister?" Alison cries out again. Before she has finished asking the same question a second time, I hold up a finger to the nurse, indicating I need a minute with my sister.

"I'll be back," promises the nurse as I duck into Alison's hospital room.

"Here I am," I announce cheerfully, as if I'm part of a magic act and have leaped out of a hat or from inside a black box with swords sticking out in all directions. I cut her off in mid-rant and rush to the side of her hospital bed. Bending over the rail, I give her a kiss on the side of her face. My lips feel as if they have touched thin parchment laid to rest in a museum vault for hundreds of years. I look at LeAnn, Alison's friend from Kanab, who is standing opposite me on the other side of the bed; we nod. I struggle to compose my face to hide the shock at my little sister's decline in just the last two weeks. Guilt rises inside of me. I should not have returned to Vermont.

In the two weeks since I was with Alley in Kanab, she has gone from an old woman prematurely wrinkled by alcohol and smoking to a glacial mummy. There is nothing to her. Not an ounce of fat or muscle is visible anywhere on her. Her skin is now as tight to her bones as a surgical glove. Her head is smaller, all eyes and mouth, making her look more like one of Jim Henson's Muppets—except, unlike the adorable puppets, Alison's face is spotted with bruises and sores. What the hell is wrong with her? Does she have cancer? AIDS?

"There you are," she says between spoonfuls of vanilla yogurt. LeAnn is patiently waiting, holding the full spoon in midair. Alley opens her mouth again like a hungry baby bird, and LeAnn gently places the spoon between her lips, tilts up the handle, and slides it back out.

"I love your hair," says Alley after swallowing. Her voice sounds strained and weak. Her words and inflection are those of a child who is surprised to see you when you uncover your own eyes. "Will you cut my hair to look like yours?" she asks.

My sister looks like a concentration-camp survivor, and she is asking to have her hair cut like mine. She has no idea what she has done to herself or how she looks.

"Sure," I say without thinking. I can't pull my eyes away from the wreck lying in the hospital bed. She looks all wrong. Her teeth and eyes are way too large for her face. Her nose is too narrow, and her ears are just all wrong. She looks as if she has been assembled from spare parts.

"I want my hair cut like yours. Can you color my hair the same color?" Her huge eyes totally focus on me as mine are on her.

"Sure," I repeat. "But I think we have to wait for your hair to grow out a little." I run my fingers through her hair the way my stylist does when I first sit down in the chair and she asks what we are going to do with it today.

"Okay, but will you color my hair the same as yours?" My fingers are still playing with her hair. "I want mine the same color as yours."

"I can do that," I assure my sister. "What color?" Every time I visited Alley in Kanab, she would ask me to color her hair, and I would always ask what color she wanted. She would always say "Surprise me."

"I want it the same color as yours," she tells me again. "When?" With the determination of a four-year-old, Alley keeps her eyes fixed to my face, expecting me to give her the exact time that this event will take place. She smiles at me, glad I am here; gone and forgotten is all the venomous anger of just fourteen days ago.

"When will you color my hair?" she demands to know.

"Ah …" I hesitate as I will myself to think. "Let's just get you out of here first, and then I will color it."

"Okay," Alley agrees in a rare moment of compliance. "Did you buy the first-class tickets for tomorrow? Are we leaving in the morning? You said if I stayed in the hospital and did as I was told, you would take me back to Vermont when you got here."

"Honey, first we have to talk to your doctor." I reach over the bed rail to touch her hand. Her hands, motionless since I walked into the room, do not respond to my gentle squeeze.

"Then we can go to Vermont?" Alison asks with the anticipation of a toddler on Christmas Eve.

"As soon as he says you are strong enough to travel, we will fly back to Vermont."

"You said I could have a first-class ticket, so I will be more comfortable," she reminds me again. "When are we leaving?"

"Yep, you will have a first-class ticket, I promise." Seeing her now, so thin, I am worried that this may be the first promise I've made to my sister that I will not be able to keep. "We will leave as soon as your doctor says you are strong enough to travel. Alley, I bought a one-way ticket here, and I won't leave without you. We will leave together."

"Okay, but will you dye my hair?" she asks. She is like a child on Christmas morning dashing between new presents, too excited to focus on any one of them.

"Yes, I will dye your hair," I say again. But she has lost interest in her hair and is instead looking over my head. I turn and see the soundless television mounted on the wall. As silently as a ghost, a golfer strolls across the links and crouches behind his ball.

"Tiger isn't playing today. He is having surgery in this hospital. I saw him in the hall," she says, taking me completely by surprise. Her eyes don't waver from the screen. She is totally captivated by the slow action on the putting green. I have been forgotten, along with her hair and her first-class ticket. I take advantage of being overlooked and circle to the other side of the hospital bed to give LeAnn a hug.

"Thanks for being here. I am really happy to see you," I tell Alison's only real friend in Kanab. The two of them have been friends since LeAnn moved in across the street. For the past six or seven years, they have looked after one another's pets and houses when one or the other went out of town.

"No need to thank me," she says, giving me a smile. "She's really happy you are here. She has been talking about how you are coming to take her back to Vermont." LeAnn raises her eye brows silently asking if it is now possible to take her home. "Can I get you something to eat? There is a cafeteria downstairs."

The head nurse curls her finger at me, beckoning me to meet her in the hall. "I have to talk to the nurse for a minute first. I will be right back." I say this softly to avoid distracting Alison from the golf game while still reassuring her that I am not leaving.

"I will stay here with Alley while you talk to the nurse, and then I will get you something to eat," LeAnn promises. I am so grateful for this gentle friend who is more comfortable in hiking boots and a backpack than heels and a handbag. She and Alison share a love of the environment, photography, and animals.

When I was here two weeks ago, LeAnn and I talked over Mexican food about what would be the best decision for Alison.

The best, we decided, was for Alison to go home to Vermont with me. I have my friends in Vermont, and my children would also pitch in. It was difficult for me to fly back and forth to see Alison on a regular basis, and her friends in Kanab have jobs. When I am at home, I talk to either Alley or LeAnn at least once every day. Sometimes I talk to both of them.

"Thanks, LeAnn. Be right back."

"No need to thank me—and take your time. I will be right here with Alley." Still holding the vanilla yogurt and plastic spoon, LeAnn says to my sister, "Alley, you want more yogurt?"

Alison opens her mouth in response to the offer. I turn and slowly head for the door. My sister's simian eyes move from the soundless television and follow me to the door. Her face bears the same wide-eyed look my little son would give me as I paced around his hospital room after his hip surgery more than twenty years ago.

"I will be right here," I say, pointing to a spot just beyond the threshold between her room and the hall. The nurse steps back out of sight and earshot of Alison. I follow, keeping my hand wrapped around the edge of the jamb so my sister will know I have not left.

"Your sister has been waiting for you. We have, too," she says in a brisk, professional tone. I search her face for any blame. Is this where she is going to tell me my sister is now mine to take care of and is no longer their problem? I know this show. I have performed in this drama during prime time, late at night, and over morning coffee, and the name of the show is always the same: *Linda to the Rescue.* The script is always the same. In this show, I have driven my father to detoxification and hunted my brother down to find him in a drug haze. I have stood by Alison through four DUIs and countless breakups of toxic relationships. And through it all, there is no one I have wanted to rescue more than my little sister.

"Your sister says you are coming to take her back to Vermont. Are you really going to take her back to Vermont?"

What does she mean, am I taking Alison back to Vermont? Of course I am taking her back. What don't I know? "Am I?" I ask wearily. She wastes no time on small talk, and neither do I.

"I don't think she will ever leave the hospital." Her face relaxes as she gives me time to process this statement.

"I want to take her home. I want to admit her to the hospital in Burlington, where I can see her and take care of her." I cast a mental net to pull my thoughts together. "She has lost so much weight since I was here two weeks ago." I have always known what to do before, what action I need to take. Now I am not so sure.

I have been taking care of Alison off and on during her life since I was too young to know I was too young to be my sister's mother.

"I don't know what the problem is," I say to the nurse and to myself.

The nurse gives me a warm smile. "Your sister is happy you are here. She talks about you all day. Actually, you are all she talks about. We are happy you are here, too." She touches my arm. "I'll come back in a little while." She takes a step back and turns. "Oh," she says, turning back around to face me. "Don't sit on the bed—there are sensors under the pad, and an alarm will go off when you get up."

"Thanks for the warning."

"I want coffee and I want chicken and I want a salad … and … and … and …" I hear Alison demand.

"You want all that?" I ask Alley, reentering the room. I look at my sister, and I just want to ask her why. *Why did you do this to yourself? Why did you do this to me? How could I have let this happen?* Maybe the nurse is wrong, and I can get her back to Vermont and put her in the medical center in Burlington. She can live with me. My children live nearby, and I know they will help me take care of their aunt, and I have my friends there.

"I want coffee and chicken and mashed potatoes." Alison is smiling; she is enjoying the idea of lots of food. If LeAnn finds chicken and mashed potatoes, will Alison actually eat them?

"Linda," says LeAnn, stepping around the bed, "I'll run down and get something for Alley. What do you want to eat? You must be hungry."

I hesitate for a moment. "I'll just eat what Alley doesn't. Thanks."

I watch as LeAnn leaves the room and then turn back to my sister. I have been going at mach speed getting ready to leave home, not knowing how long I would be gone. I put my old, dear black Lab to sleep three days ago. I tutored my son on the care and feeding of our surviving old, sick dog and scrubbed the house. Then I sat in an airport or plane for about ten hours to get to Alison. Now what are we going to do? Not being able to get her back to Vermont wasn't something I had considered.

Alison has always sought adventure. She loves the spur of the moment. Me, I have to plan everything. When I was about to turn forty, I resolved to conquer my fear of heights by going skydiving on my birthday. My sister, ever supportive, said she would give it to me as an early birthday present. I set the date and invited some friends.

Alley showed up to remind me that being on a ski lift makes me anxious; this comment got laughs. The pilot announced there was room for one more skydiver and asked if there were any takers. Alison leaped into a blue jumpsuit. On the way up, I considered returning with the plane but decided I would be too embarrassed. Alley, on the other hand, was so excited she somersaulted out the airplane's door, screaming and laughing. My sister knows no fear.

I was so frightened, the guy I was attached to had to give me step-by-step instructions and then peel my hands off the metal supports under the wing.

Turning back to Alison now, who is staring at the perfectly manicured greens on the television, I wonder when she lost her enjoyment of trying new things and going to new places.

"Here we are," announces LeAnn with the exaggerated cheerfulness reserved for small kids and the elderly. In her arms she carries a cardboard takeout box filled with food from the hospital's cafeteria. "I didn't know what to get, so I got a bunch of stuff," she explains. "And for you, Alley, I got coffee and some pudding and some yogurt and—"

Alley changes her focus from the golf show to "the LeAnn show" as easily as one changes television channels.

"I want coffee! I want coffee! I want coffee!" Alley says over and over with excitement. Her enthusiasm is incongruous with the wrinkled, dry skin and the thinning hair. Her body is prepubescent in its size and shape and could be mistaken for that of a young boy. But her face gives her away. It is the face of a very old person.

LeAnn puts down the box, takes out a cup of coffee, and adds milk. She holds the straw to Alison's lips.

"Good … that is soooo good." Alley says in a thick voice. "I want chicken and mashed potatoes." Alison doesn't make eye contact with either LeAnn or me. Her eyes shift back to the television screen and the perfectly manicured golf green. She makes no effort to reach for the food or to feed herself. Her bruised hands just lie on the bed at her sides. Passivity has never been a part of my sister's behavior before. She has always been in motion. If she wasn't working, she was mowing the lawn or stacking wood or driving around looking for photo opportunities.

While LeAnn held the coffee cup, I got out the requested chicken and mashed potatoes. "You want to try a little mashed potato?" I ask Alison. Her mouth opens, and I feed her a spoonful of potatoes. She doesn't take her attention from the television. She does not look at me or the food.

"That's so good," she groans with total pleasure. "That is soooo good." Her mouth opens again to accept another spoonful.

"Linda, I'll feed her, and you can eat," offers LeAnn.

I move back to the couch, and Alison's friend and neighbor takes my place at my sister's side and gives her another spoonful. After a couple of bites, Alley doesn't open her mouth. She has had enough, just like when she was a little girl sitting next to me in her high chair.

When we were little, Mother would put dinner on the table, set Alison in her high chair next to me, and leave the kitchen. My sister was my child to feed.

LeAnn rips open a vanilla yogurt, stirs it, and tempts Alley by holding a spoonful in front of her mouth. Her mouth opens. She takes a few spoonfuls of the yogurt before refusing to open her mouth again.

Just as I am eating another piece of chicken, the physical therapist shows up to help Alley go for her second walk of the day. Just the sight of the young woman causes Alison to start protesting in a harsh, strained voice: "No, no, no!"

My sister's vulnerability brings me to tears, and I can't swallow.

"She hated this yesterday, too," comments LeAnn. "She screamed and cried—said she was afraid of falling."

The therapist pulls back the blanket and sheet covering Alison as she attempts to ease my sister's anxiety. "Alison, you are fine. I am not going to let you fall," she says, speaking slowly.

"Alley, we won't let you fall," I say, doubling up on the promise of safety. I put my cardboard box of chicken and potatoes down on the couch next to me and go to Alison's side.

"She really needs to do this herself," instructs the PT, who is standing directly in front of Alley. "Come on, Alison. You did this yesterday. We are all here to help you, but you need to do this yourself."

"I can't. No," cries Alley. "I can't."

"Yes, you can," she coaxes. She sounds as if she is talking to someone in their nineties. My sister isn't old; she's my younger sister. She is only fifty-four. I have just traveled through four airports and three time zones, and Alison sobs and begs to be left alone because she has to walk the three feet between her bed and the chair. There is a helplessness about Alley I have never seen before. After much screaming and sobbing and protests of, "I can't," Alley makes it to the chair.

"Alison, I will be back in a couple of hours to help you get back into bed," says the PT, draping a blanket over her patient's tiny body.

I sit down heavily on the couch in front of the large window next to the recliner where Alison sits motionlessly, staring at the television. Her hands lie lifelessly in her lap on top of the light blue thermal hospital blanket.

Tiger strolls onto the green and sinks a long putt. "This must be an old game, because he is here in the hospital," says Alison without taking her eyes off the screen. The traumatic transition from the bed to the chair is now ancient history, a distant memory.

I don't answer. I don't tell her Tiger is not in St. George, Utah. I don't ask her how she feels. I don't ask her if she wants anything. I sit on the couch and stare at my sister. I have never seen anyone like this before; I can't believe she has done this to herself. My eyes move from her bony fingers to her too thin face. She is completely unaware of me staring at her.

"Linny, I'm going to head out," LeAnn says. She walks over to Alley and touches her arm. "Alley, I am going home now. I will check on Dax and Marco. See you tomorrow." Dax and Marco Polo are Alison's cats.

"Okay," Alison says, not looking at her friend. She never takes her eyes from the television screen.

The same nurse with whom I had chatted outside the door takes advantage of the empty bed and yanks off the sheets. She tells me the shift will be changing shortly and that the doctor will be here to talk to me in the morning. I had hoped to talk to the doctor tonight. I will have to wait.

She leaves the room, returning in seconds with fresh sheets, two towels, and a face cloth and a handful of toiletries. "I brought you a few things," she tells me as she stocks the bathroom with deodorant, shampoo, a comb, a toothbrush, and toothpaste.

"Wow, thanks," I mumble, embarrassed by her thoughtfulness. I had not expected this. I don't feel as if I deserve her kindness.

"The couch folds into a bed," the nurse says as she flips the back cushion down.

"I can do that," I tell her quickly. She ignores my protests, and soon enough, like those people who turn ordinary balloons into animals, she has it all made up with sheets, a blanket, and a pillow. Then, together, we remake my sister's bed.

The nurse looks at me across the hospital bed and says, "She is really glad you are here. Have a good night. I will see you in the morning." She disappears.

I am out of practice at accepting things being done for me. I remind myself to thank her properly tomorrow.

Exhausted, I slump down on my newly made bed next to Alison's chair and watch her watching the soundless television. "Alley, you want anything?"

"No." She answers without looking at me. Alley doesn't ask about when we are leaving. I lean back and allow my body to relax into the cushion.

True to her word and with an efficiency driven by a demanding schedule, the PT walks back into the room and tells Alison it is time to get back into her bed.

"No," Alison whines. She closes her eyes; maybe if she can't see the PT, she is not there. She hasn't the strength to offer any real objection to whatever is happening to her.

"She really doesn't like to do this," the physical therapist reminds me. She pulls the blanket from Alison's lap—my sister's only defense, her only perceived protection. Alley's fingers make a grabbing motion in an attempt to keep the blanket from being taken from her. There is nothing else. Even her big sister is not preventing this attack. The futility of the gesture is pathetic and sad. My sister's frailness is hard to look at. I would be sad, but more accepting, if this were my grandmother in front of me. But she isn't; this breakable-looking sixty-three-pound person is my baby sister.

"No, no, no!" she cries repeatedly. "Please, no. No! Leave me alone." Her cries are ignored as the PT and I lower the footrest and help my sister to sit up.

"Alison, we are going to help you to stand up and walk over to the bed." The PT is adamant that my sister is going to walk from the chair to her bed, but she is not without compassion.

"No, no, no! You will drop me. I can't do this. Please stop. No. I can't! You will drop me." Helplessness has replaced the strength that had once carried an eighty-pound pack through the Teton Mountains, kayaked the Alaskan coast, climbed Kilimanjaro, and served a tennis ball that made my racquet spin in my grip.

"Alison, your sister and I are going to slide you closer to the edge, so your feet can touch the floor." The PT ignored my sister's cries, which were nothing short of gut-wrenching. "You're doing great, Alison—just a little farther, and then we can get you on your feet."

I go to the other side to give her support. But I want to tell her to stop crying, and I want to plead with the PT to see that my sister isn't strong enough, and we should not carry her … but how is she going to return to Vermont if she is so frightened to move three feet?

"Don't drop me! Don't drop me!" she begs us. We are on either side of her, each with one arm under hers with the other around her waist. There is no way we will allow her to fall. "Help me! Help me!" She is more terrified than I have ever seen her before.

"You're fine—you are doing great," encourages the PT in a voice that engenders confidence.

"Honey, you're doing great," I confirm. "Just one more step," I tell her, trying to make it sound as if we only have time for one more run down a black-diamond trail at Mount Mansfield. With tag team praise, we coax my little sister back to her bed and its fresh sheets.

Now, it is just the two of us. I take up a position at my sister's bedside with my hand on the rail. The lights in the hall dim, signaling an end to the hectic business of healing and providing a cue to settle in for the night.

I look at Alley. "Honey, do you need—want—anything?" I ask her.

"No."

"You want to watch TV?"

"No."

"Do you mind if I watch the news?"

"Where is my phone? I need my cell phone."

"Who do you need to call?" I stand up and look around her bed, searching for her cell phone. I didn't even know she had a cell phone. "Why do you need your phone? Who do you need to call?"

"I need to call Michelle."

"Who is Michelle?

"The smoothie lady."

"What?"

"I need to call Michelle. I want a fruit smoothie."

"Do you want more yogurt? I will get you one."

"No," Alley says with all her energy to express her frustration.

"Alley, who is Michelle?"

"The smoothie lady," she huffs. "She makes the best fruit smoothies."

"Where is she?" I find the phone pinned in the pocket of her robe, check her contacts, and find a number for Michelle. I recognize the area code: Kanab.

"In Kanab! Alison, you can't ask Michelle in the middle of the night to make you a smoothie and drive two hours to bring it to you and then two hours back to Kanab."

"She will do it for me," Alley insists.

"Alley, maybe she will, but you can't ask someone to do that."

"Yes, I can. She won't mind. She will do that for me."

"Alison!" I don't know what to say. I am totally blown away by my sister's lack of consideration.

"She will bring me a smoothie." Her agitation is increasing; she wants her own way no matter what.

I know that by the time the smoothie lady arrives, Alley will have forgotten all about asking for the fruit concoction.

"Alley …" I soften my voice. I can't blame her for wanting to feel loved. Mommies make their sick children special things like smoothies and hot chocolate. Mommies sit and rock their children when they are sad or have scraped their knees or when their favorite teddy bear has gone missing. And when our children call because their hearts have just been broken over the end of a relationship, mommies listen and remind them that it takes two, and they can't take all the blame. Mommies say "I love you" and remind their children of their wonderful qualities and achievements.

Alison had had too little of the special foods, and sitting on mother's lap, being rocked. When her heart was broken, she could not go to Mother for comfort over the loss of a female lover. Mother would never accept or believe her younger daughter was a lesbian.

"She makes the best smoothies. I saw him in the hospital."

"Al, I am sure she makes the best smoothies in the world. She will make you one when we get back to Kanab. Who? Who did you see in the hospital?"

"Tiger. I saw him."

"Where?"

"He is here in the hospital," Alison insists.

"Why is he here?" I am not as concerned with Tiger Woods's health as I am about my little sister. I want her to have comfort foods and favorite books read to her and someone to be at her beck and call.

"He had an operation," she answers.

"Al, do you want anything to eat?"

"Coffee. I want coffee."

I walk out into the hall to ask where I can get some coffee, and a friendly nurse says he will bring it to me. He returns in minutes with coffee, a small carton of milk, vanilla ice cream, Jell-O, applesauce, pudding, and vanilla yogurt.

"Thought you might need these," he says.

"Thank you very much." I take a few sips of the black coffee rather than wasting it by pouring half of it down the drain. I fill the space with milk to dilute the coffee. Popping in a straw, I hold it to Alley's lips.

"Soooo good," she mumbles between sips.

"Alley, do you want anything else?" I sweep my eyes over the tray again and let her know her choices. "How about some Jell-O, or ice cream, or applesauce, or yogurt, or pudding, or …"

"Pudding. I want vanilla pudding."

"This is your lucky day," I tell her with a smile as I peel back the lid from the plastic cup. "You want to feed yourself?" I offer her the spoon to see if she will move her hand.

"No."

"You want me to feed you?" I stir the pudding. Alley doesn't answer; she just opens her month and waits for me to feed her the way I did when she was a baby. But I am not six years old, and she is not one. I am fifty-nine, and Alley is fifty-four. It isn't supposed to happen like this. I have always imagined us together, watching *Law and Order*, when I am eighty nine and Alley is eighty four.

The nurse comes in and takes Alison's vitals. "We need to pull you up a little; you're sliding down your bed," he says, using the power control to lower the head of the bed. With one of us on either side, we pull her up toward the top of the bed.

"You okay?" I ask her while the nurse takes her blood pressure.

"I need … I need …"

"What do you need?" My tone is gentle.

"I need … I need …"

"What do you need?"

"I need … I need …"

"Alley, I am going to just sit and watch the news for a few minutes. I will be right here in case you need something."

"Okay, you watch the news."

I change the channel to CNN and lie down on my converted bed. Alison's eyes are closed, and I think that she has finally gone to sleep. I allow my exhaustion to reach my consciousness. Still dressed in the clothes I traveled in all day, I curl up on the couch and pull the blanket over me.

"Linny, I want … I want … I want …"

I jump up and go to the side of her bed. "Alley, what do you want?"

"I want … I want … I want …"

"Alley, what do you want?" I lean over the rail, lowering my head close to my sister. "Honey, what do you need?"

"I need … I need … I need …"

"Alley, what do you need?" I whisper.

She doesn't answer. I return to the couch and roll onto my side, facing my sister.

"Linny, I need … I need …"

I take a big breath and release it. If I don't say anything, maybe she will stop calling for me.

"I need … I need … I need …"

Without getting up, I ask, "Alley, what do you need?"

"I need … I need …"

I don't know if she knows she is saying this. I get up and go to her bedside. "Alison, tell me what you need."

"What?" She looks at me in complete surprise. I don't think she knows she has been calling out.

"Honey, I really need to go to sleep," I tell her. "I am really tired."

"Okay, Linny, you go to sleep. Good night," she says with a tender thoughtfulness that takes me a little by surprise.

"Good night, Alley." I give her a kiss on her forehead.

I lie back down, pull the blanket over me, and close my eyes.

"I need … I need … I want … I want … I need …"

I roll over facing the back of the couch.

"I need … I need … I need …"

Chapter Two

Two nights before I was scheduled to return to Kanab to visit my sister, I received a phone call from Gary, a social worker from the emergency room at Kane County Hospital in Kanab, Utah.

"Are you Alison Booth's sister, Linda?" asked the male voice in the middle of my night.

"Yes, I am Linda, and Alison Booth is my sister." I sat up quickly and turned on the Chinese lamp next to my bed. A feeling of panic rose up from my gut into my throat. Had something happened to Alison? Recently, I talked to her every day; some days, I talked to her twice. I had just talked to her the night before. She had finally said she wanted to come live with me. My doctor would see her as soon as she arrived.

Alison even promised me she would go to the medical center in Burlington. It would be hard for her, because she wouldn't be able to smoke in the hospital.

"Linda," the social worker said, bringing me back to why Alison was in the emergency room. "Alison's neighbor, LeAnn Skrz … Skrz …"

"Yes, I know LeAnn." I had just talked to Alison. I had just talked to LeAnn. How could this be? We had made a plan just three or four hours before. I was going to fly out to Utah and bring my sister back to Vermont. She was going to live with me. I had already bought a one-way ticket to Utah. A friend was going to arrange the first-class seats as soon as Alley was ready to travel back to Vermont.

"LeAnn found your sister lying on the floor in her home. Alison appears to be confused and suffering from dehydration and malnutrition and hasn't had a bath. She … she is really dirty."

How can she be dirty? I wondered. *She washes herself all over with witch hazel. She has a thing about being clean. When I was there she wanted me to give her a shower and wash her hair every other day while she sat on a plastic stool in the bathtub.*

"We want to transfer her to Dixie Regional Medical Hospital in St. George, but she refuses to go. She is refusing all medical care."

"Why?" I blurted out. I sat up straighter on the edge of my bed.

"She says that you are coming on Sunday and taking her back to Vermont, and when she gets to Vermont everything will be fine. Is that true?"

"Oh my God." *What have I done? I shouldn't have left her there alone. I wish so much I hadn't left.*

"Linda," said the social worker, pulling me back to the present, "are you coming out here and taking Alison back to Vermont?" His voice was calm and patient.

"Yes, yes—I have a ticket for Sunday. I arrive at 4:40 p.m. in St. George." I allowed my head to fall into my open palm as I sat on the edge of my bed. With my other hand, I held the phone tight against my ear.

"Then you are you planning to take her back to Vermont?"

"My plan is to …" I stopped in midsentence. I had been so focused on my plan that I hadn't realized it might not happen. "Yes, I plan to bring her back, and I have already spoken to a doctor here in Burlington. He will see her right away." I was talking fast. Was I trying to convince Gary that I really was a good sister, or convince myself everything would be fine? I never would have left if I had known she was that sick. I was feeling guilty. "Do you think I should not bring her back to Vermont?"

"Right now," began Gary slowly, "Alison is so sick she needs to be transferred to the hospital in St. George. She says she doesn't have to go. She thinks she will be fine once she is back in Vermont. We would like to send her in an ambulance, but she is refusing." The social worker stopped talking, either to give me an opportunity to say something or ask a question. I couldn't think of anything to say. Maybe he was just trying to figure out how to say something else—something even more horrible.

"If she doesn't go," he began again, "I ..." I could feel him weighing his words. "I am not sure she will survive the night."

My body went rigid. "Can I talk to her?" I asked.

"I will have to go back into the treatment room and call you back. Give me a few minutes to get there." He doesn't hang up. "Linda ..." he began hesitantly. "You should know that your sister has threatened people here in the hospital."

"What do you mean, threatened? How can she hurt anyone?" This was unbelievable. *Alison, hurt someone? No!*

"She is saying she will shoot someone. Does she own a gun?"

"Yes, she has a small .22 pistol," I admitted. "But she is in no condition to hurt anyone right now. She will say anything that comes into her head." No one knew better than I did the kinds of meanness that could come out of her mouth. "I will have LeAnn remove the gun from the house," I continued with assurance. "I think the reason she does not want to go to the hospital in St. George is because she will not be able to smoke."

"The doctor has already put a patch on her. Linda, give me a few minutes to walk back to the treatment room."

I hung up the phone and sat on the edge of my bed, waiting for him to call me back. My flight wasn't for two days. *I could change my flight and reschedule my doctor's appointment for tomorrow. If only I could beam myself there.* The phone rang.

"Hello?"

21

"Linda, here's Alison," said the now-familiar caring voice.

"Hi, Alley. What—"

"Linny, I don't need to go to St. George." My little sister's voice was weak and pleading. I wiped tears from my cheeks with the hand not holding the phone. I didn't want to lose my sister.

"Alley, Gary says that—"

"I don't want to go to St. George. I want to go home."

"Alison, yeah, you do need to go to St. George." I used my best mothering voice, an authoritative tone mixed with a softer bit of "this is for your own good."

"But you are coming to get me and take me to your doctor in Burlington. Aren't you?" Any anger I had felt about Alley when I was in Kanab disappeared at the sound of her helplessness. My little sister was defeated and broken; she had nothing left to fight with. She just wanted to feel safe and loved, and I was not there to hold her, to feed her. I wanted to sit in a rocking chair with her on my lap and tell her stories. I wanted to promise her that she was going to be okay. Right then, I had to convince her that going to St. George would make her okay.

"Alley, yes, I am coming to get you and take you to see Chris, so—"

"When? When are you coming to take me to see Chris?"

Her voice was so sad. I took a deep breath. I needed to reassure her that she was going to be okay, and she needed to go to St. George.

"Alley," I said quietly, using her childhood name to get her attention. "I'll be there on Sunday, in two days, at 4:40 at the St. George Airport, and then—"

"And then you will take me to Vermont? Does K have the ticket? Did she get me a first-class ticket, so I will be comfortable?"

"Alison, I will be in St. George on Sunday, and then I will go to the hospital. But first, I need for you to go to the hospital in St. George."

"I want to go home." There was no more, bratty child demanding to have things her way. She was more like a wounded animal trying to crawl away to someplace familiar and safe.

"Honey, I need you to go to the hospital, so you will be stronger for the trip back to Vermont." I couldn't let her argue with me about this. Her life depended on her getting into the ambulance.

I tried again. "Alley." I checked my tone to be sure it was calm, but firm. I resisted telling her to do as I said, because I didn't want her to rebel and do the opposite. "Alley, I will bring you back to Vermont with me, but first, I need you to go to St. George in the ambulance." I heard her start to protest again, but I interrupted this time. "Alley, I love you, and I know this is going to be hard for you, because you will not be able to smoke in the hospital."

"No, it won't. I don't have to smoke." The unspoken "so there" was clear. She'd been smoking three packs a day for thirty years. I hadn't meant it as a dare, but if it worked, then good.

"I know it is hard," I repeated, "but Alley, I need … *I need*"—I had emphasized the "I need" so I would sound less demanding— "for you to go to the hospital in St. George, so you will be strong enough to fly back to Vermont with me. I will be there on Sunday."

"You are taking me home the next day, right?" I could hear her crying. My once strong, athletic sister was so helpless and fragile. The woman who could outhike, outswim, and outski me, and then kill me on the tennis court, believed I could make her all better. She needed to believe I could make her all better.

"You will take me home the next day, right?" Alley pressed me for certainty. I didn't want to make a promise I couldn't keep.

"Alley, you and I will have to talk to the doctor first. As soon as he says you are strong enough to fly, K will buy the tickets for you and me to fly back to Vermont. I bought a one-way ticket to St. George, so the only way I am leaving is with you. Okay? As soon as we get all the information we need, we will fly back to my house."

"Alison, listen," I continued quickly to keep her attention and preempt any further protests. "I need for you to be stronger to make the trip back to Vermont. You need to go to the hospital tonight. I know this will be hard for you, because you will not be able to smoke."

I needed to keep challenging her on the smoking, because three weeks ago I had taken Alison to the hospital in Kanab to receive nutrition through an IV, and she had called me three hours into a five-and-a-half-hour intravenous drip to come and get her. When I told her she needed to stay, she got nasty and yelled, "Come! Get! Me!" I drove into the circle by the main entrance, and she was already outside sitting in a wheelchair. Getting out of the car, I ran around to help her into the passenger seat. By the time I had walked back around and gotten behind the wheel, she was lighting a cigarette from the car's lighter.

Her defiant four-year-old voice came to me through the phone, shaking me from the memory. "I cannot smoke."

"Okay, good, then. I need you to go and do everything the doctor asks you to do, so you will be stronger."

"I can do that," she said with conviction.

"You need to stay in the hospital until I get there. I will be there on Sunday."

"Linny, I will do what you tell me to do. If you tell me to go to the hospital and stay until you get there, I will." Alley was starting to sound very sleepy. "Then, on Monday, we will fly to Vermont."

"Alison, I have a one-way ticket to Utah, and I will not leave Utah without you," I told her again. "I promise."

"Whatever you say—I will do whatever you say. Then you will take me to Vermont." It was no longer a question. We were making progress.

"Yes, I will take you to Vermont. When I get there on Sunday, we will make a plan. Okay?"

"Okay, we will make a plan on Sunday," Alison parroted.

It had only been two weeks since I had been at my sister's house. During the two and a half weeks I was there, Alison had been impossible. Between the blaring television, her nonstop smoking, and the medical alert going off all night long, I did not get much sleep. During the night, she would roll over and set off the medical alert that hung around her neck, and then the phone would ring. I told the man on the phone I was her sister, and she was fine. After the third time in one night, he asked me to remove it.

Most mornings would find her sitting on the couch in the living room with the television on at maximum volume. As if that weren't enough, there was the plethora of wind chimes hanging from the one shaggy bark tree in her backyard or the roof overhang or bracket screwed into the house. Closing the window and door to the guest room was of no use. I would finally get up and make coffee for us. One morning, I found her watching a Josh Groban DVD. Tears gushed down her face as she waved her hands high above her head. She was conducting the orchestra.

"Isn't this so beautiful?" she said with emotion when she saw me.

"Yes, it is," I mumbled. There was no point in getting upset. I placed a cup of coffee beside her on the antique gun case she used as an end table. Then I sat down on the other end of the couch holding my cup of coffee between both of my hands. The morning air in the desert was chilly, and Alley was wearing nothing but a tank top and men's boxer shorts. It was only 4:30 a.m.

The music stopped, and without getting up, Alison switched back to the television. "More milk," she demanded. Her tone was aggressive and angry.

Without saying a word, I stood, picked up her cup, returned to the kitchen, added a little more milk, and took it back to her.

"Here you go," I said, covering my irritation with a smile. Her eyes didn't leave the screen, and she said nothing.

She surfed through the channels, clinging to the remote control absentmindedly, and I got the impression she was not really looking for anything in particular.

"Alley, can you put on *The Today Show*?" I asked.

"No." My sister leaned forward slowly and struggled to pull a cigarette from the pack. I just watched as she put it between her lips and then reached for the disposable lighter. In the ashtray on the couch lay a cigarette with a thin stream of smoke rising up between us. After taking a shallow draw—just enough to burn the end—she laid it down in the same ashtray. Her hand brushed the first, sending it rolling across the faux sheepskin she was sitting on.

With all the casualness of a talk-show host, I picked it up and carried it to the kitchen, where I held it under the faucet. *Christ, this isn't how I want to die. I have to say something. I have to talk to her again about going back to Vermont with me.*

I refilled my coffee and walked around the half wall dividing the kitchen and living room. Alison was hitting the up button on the remote in a steady rhythm, as if she were listening to a metronome. The channels flashed by like a slide show.

"Alley," I began slowly. She turned her large eyes in my direction, and her gaze locked on my face. "Alley, I want you to come back to Vermont with me."

She continued to stare at me for what felt like a very long time.

"No," she finally said.

"Alley, you need to see a doctor. We need to find out what is wrong with you." She turned back to the slide show. "Alison, you need to see a doctor. You can't go on like this." My words fell on deaf ears. "Alison," I said more loudly, trying to get her attention. "Alison, you are all I have. Please—"

"Don't talk shit!" she yelled, interrupting me.

Two days before, I had taken her to her doctor's appointment in Kanab. The doctor weighed her and asked how she felt. "Fine" was her answer.

"Okay," he said. "Drink a couple of Ensures a day to put back on some weight."

That's all? I thought. *Is that all he has to say when his patient weighs less than eighty pounds?* I took her home and told her I had to go to the store, and I returned to the medical offices at the hospital.

"What is wrong with her?" I demanded to know once I was back inside the office and the door was closed.

I sat down in a chair in front of the window, and the doctor half sat on the end of the examination table.

"I don't know," the young, white-coated doctor confessed. "Your sister won't allow us to do any tests."

"What?" I wanted to yell and say, *How can you not know what is wrong with her? She weighs seventy-three pounds and looks like one of those dolls whose heads are made from a dried apple!* "She told me she had a pinched nerve."

"She won't allow us to do any tests to find out what is wrong," he repeated.

Oh, my God, I thought. "What is your best guess?" I asked with a hint of panic in my voice.

"My best guess is that she has cancer, but I don't know."

Okay ... now what? I had raised two kids since they were very small, and I had done it totally on my own, so I could do this. I just needed to find out what was wrong and fix it. "What do we need to do?" I asked the doctor. I was all about setting goals and making plans of action.

"Because she won't allow us to run any tests, there is really nothing I can do. I have prescribed Ensure twice a day and insisted she come in daily for IV fluids. She won't come. She is an adult, and if she refuses treatment, there is nothing we can do."

"She is sick," I insisted. "There has to be a way to insist on treatment."

"You would need to prove that she is incapable of making decisions for herself, and that would take time. You would need to show that Alison is incompetent in the state of Utah."

It was not an easy thing to take away another person's rights. Alison had said many times that if she were ever really sick, she would refuse treatment and just die. But first I needed to know what was wrong with her.

The year before, when I had taken my sister on a trip to Greece, she was so thin and frail I invited then begged her to come home with me and see a doctor. She kept insisting it was because of a pinched nerve in her back. Alley believed she was fine and the weight loss looked good on her. I drove home from Montreal without her.

She refused. She was adamant that she had to go home to her cats. I said I would call her neighbor LeAnn and have her take care of them. For each excuse Alley threw out, I had a remedy. In the end, all I could do was take her luggage home with me so she would not have to cope with it when she went through customs at LAX. I washed everything, repacked it perfectly in her suitcase, and mailed it to her in a large box.

I left the doctor's office. I had wanted him to tell me she had cancer or some other disease. I wanted to put a name to it. With a diagnosis, I would have a way to talk about it—and a treatment to talk her into. I would know what needed to be done. I needed some way to understand her sudden difficulty with reading; she had been a great reader. If something were wrong in her brain, it would explain her inability to follow the plot of a sitcom.

I would have to prove in a court of law that she was incompetent to make her own decisions. It would take months, the doctor had explained. By then, she would have died.

I drove to the supermarket, because that was where I had said I was going. I bought more yogurt for Alison and some bread and peanut butter for myself.

"You get lost in the ranchos again?" she asked referring to the residential area where she lived and took me years to find my way around the network of streets. I walked back into the living room and I sat down next to her with a glass of water and watched as she lit up another cigarette. I abruptly got up from the couch.

"I'm going for a walk," I told my sister. My friends on the East Coast would be home, and I needed to talk to someone other than my sister.

"Don't get lost," was her parting shot. It had been a joke from the very first time I had visited her in Kanab and got lost finding her house. I would find myself driving in circles and would find her street by chance. Then one day I smartened up and just looked for the steeple of the Mormon Temple.

It was only an excuse to be alone, a chance to think. The ranchos were quiet, with few cars. The air was clean, and the desert view seemed to go on forever.

With the heat and that altitude—more than seven thousand feet above sea level—my anger and frustration were spent after jogging three blocks. Vermont was only fifty feet above sea level, so I had not yet acclimated. I slowed to a walk and pulled out my cell phone to call my friends Mike and Patty.

Mike, who was also my lawyer, picked up on the second ring. "How are things going with Alison?" It was such a relief to hear his voice. He always sounded cheerful and optimistic.

"She screams at me all the time," I told him. "I'm exhausted. She keeps telling me how dumb I am. I am going to lay carpet squares in her kitchen and down the hall to her bedroom. She has fallen down a couple of times, and those are the only uncarpeted areas."

"Laying those carpet squares is harder than it looks," Mike warned me. I had watched him carpet a room in his house the previous winter, so he knew what he was talking about.

"Thanks for the warning. Anyway, she screams at me all the time. She wants her shoes lined up in front of the gas stove. She yells if they are not lined up perfectly." Then I told Mike about both of my visits to the doctor's office—first with Alison and then without her.

After a brief silence, he asked, "You sure she has cancer?"

"No, I am not sure. There is no way of knowing what is going on without performing any tests, but she's refusing them. The doctor says I would have to have her declared incompetent."

"I don't think you have time for that," Mike told me frankly. "Also, I wouldn't think that people with cancer would be too concerned about their shoes being lined up. Her obsessive behavior and weight loss sound more like Alison is anorexic to me."

Anorexic! Why hadn't I considered that? I had just never heard of someone in their fifties becoming anorexic—especially someone who had never cared about how their hair looked or how they dressed. Why would she just stop eating? She had told me she was seeing a doctor in St. George, and he thought she had a pinched nerve. What did that have to do with not eating?

After spending three days laying carpet squares to cover all the tile floors in her one-story house, I reminded my sister that I was leaving the following morning. The news seemed to jolt her from her alcoholic haze, and she drilled her eyes through me.

"Get out. Get out now!" she yelled with all the venom she could manage.

I had told her several times I would be back in two weeks to pack her things and make arrangements for her two cats. After assurances that she would be able to return to her home in Utah once she had gained weight and was healthy again she agreed. I did not believe she would ever be able to return to her adorable little stucco home in the desert.

I had talked to my doctor about seeing her. I had consulted a carpenter about enlarging the half bathroom on the first floor and converting my dining room into her bedroom. With the living room as her comfortable sitting area, the arrangement would create a small apartment for her.

I felt organized and ready to have Alison live with me. I quickly described my plans for the bathroom to Alison and explained how we could make a little apartment for her on the first floor.

"Where can I smoke?" she had asked. "You won't let me smoke in our house." She could smoke on the deck, I told her. I hoped she wouldn't ask where she could smoke when the weather got colder. Maybe she thought she would be back in her own little house.

When I'd left Kanab, I hadn't bothered to pack anything back up, because I had known I would be back shortly. I reminded her I would be back in two weeks. In anticipation of my return, I left everything I had brought, including my toiletries.

"Come back with me now," I begged her right before I left. "Come back to Vermont with me now. You can live with me like we've talked about for the past three or four years."

When she asked again where she would sleep, I thought she was finally agreeing to come with me. Then she started yelling and refusing to move from her place on the end of her couch. I left her on her own, sitting there with a drink to her left and a cigarette between the first two fingers of her right hand, and flew back to Vermont.

I called the minute I arrived back home. She was cheerful and happy to hear from me. She seemed to have forgotten she had been mad at me. It was as if her yelling at me had never happened.

Chapter Three: Day Two

I roll over on the converted couch. I don't remember going to sleep or waking up or even if I slept at all. I just know that as soon as I lay down and rolled toward the windows, Alison resumed crying, "I need … I want … help me."

Having listened to my children's cries in the night, the mother in me wouldn't allow me fall into a deep sleep. No matter how many times I got up and went to her bedside to ask what she needed or wanted, she couldn't tell me. She didn't know. She didn't know she'd cried out for help during the night. Each time, she would tell me how sorry she was for not letting me sleep. Each time, she told me she loved me. If her bed weren't booby-trapped I would have lain down next to her. Perhaps that would have comforted her into sleep.

Lying flat on my back on the couch/bed, I lift my legs up over my head and swing them forward, leveraging myself into a sitting position. I am sure I have been more tired than this, like when my son, at two, was in the hospital having his hip reconstructed, but I can't remember.

The sun is not yet up, but I can make out the dark silhouette of the large houses on the red sandstone cliffs. I know the houses are there, but in this faint light, they look like prehistoric monsters marching single file along the horizon. But it is the unidentified and unseen monsters in this room that frighten me the most.

I can't think about ancient history. I can only deal with right now. I can do nothing to change the past, be it the extinction of the giant reptiles or Alison's self-destruction. *What is wrong with Alison?*

With my hands positioned on my thighs, I shove myself to my feet. I look across the eight feet or so at my sister. Her head is turned slightly away from me. Her mouth has fallen open, and her eyes are shut. Her once-familiar profile, with the double chin and button nose, has eroded away. Now, her face is just skin laid tightly over bone and cartilage. There is nothing left. Her head is too small, her teeth too big, her nose too pointed, and the shoulders that once carried enough supplies for a month in the Grand Teton Mountains are now avian in appearance. She looks as if she will be crushed by the weight of the sheet and blanket.

I am grateful for the quiet moments before the overhead lights mark the arrival of a new day and the return of the busy business of restoring people to health and families. I can take a shower, and Alley can stay a bit longer in her dreams. Wherever she is, I hope she is not burdened by the weak sixty-three-pound body she now inhabits.

I hurry into the small corner bathroom for a quick shower. I want to be ready when the doctor arrives to check on Alison. I have a lot of questions; I need to understand what is going on—what is wrong with Alison.

I didn't bring anything with me. I left all the clothes I had planned to wear on my next trip at Alley's house, so I have to settle for a shower and a clean pair of underwear and T-shirt from my backpack. I have no choice but to wear the jeans I traveled in until we get back to her house in Kanab. Seeing the new toothbrush, deodorant, and shampoo, I am again grateful to the thoughtful nurse.

I emerge from the shower, towel-drying my hair. The massive mammoths of predawn have disappeared, and in their place are the houses I saw yesterday afternoon. I look down at Alley's sleeping face and push the hair off her forehead just to watch it fall forward again. *She wouldn't be here if Mother had cared less about her dead children and more about her living children*, I think angrily.

Why didn't I drag her back to Vermont three years ago, or even last year, on our return from Greece? I asked her to. I even begged her to get in the car before leaving Montreal.

I take my time folding the sheets and blanket and stack them neatly on the windowsill. The bed is quickly converted back into a couch, and I sit down to wait. I have a paperback book in my backpack, but I don't feel like reading.

The nurse who had been on duty all night comes in to take Alison's vitals for the last time before the day crew arrives.

"Could you use some coffee?' he asks thoughtfully. "There is a cafeteria downstairs."

"Ah …" I start to get up, but I don't want to leave Alley alone.

He understands my hesitation. "I will be in here for a while. I have a few things I have to do, really," he assures me. "Alison, your sister is going to go get some breakfast." He jerks his head toward the door wordlessly, telling me to get going. "Okay, Alison? She will be right back."

"Okay, Linny. You go get breakfast." Alison's voice is flat, as if she is reading from a script. I am not sure she understands what she is saying okay to.

"Thanks." My voice is low with fatigue and stress. "I'll be right back," I say to my sister and the nurse. I feel relief at escaping my responsibility, even if just for a few minutes. It gives me a few minutes to think about what to ask when the doctor shows up.

"Take your time," he calls after me.

"I want coffee, I want coffee, I want coffee!" chants Alley as I turn to go.

"I will get you coffee," I answer her from just outside the door.

34

"I want coffee, I want coffee, I want coffee!" I can hear my sister's voice as I head toward the elevator.

I am ready for any requests except for a smoothie, so I hope Alley doesn't remember her craving from last night. My cardboard box tray contains two coffees, some scrambled eggs, toast, yogurt, one vanilla and one strawberry, and a small carton of milk.

The nurse is just finishing up as I put my tray down on the hospital table. "Alison, I think your sister got you everything you could possibly want." He closes the portable desk and locks it. "Alison?" The nurse steps closer to get her attention. "I am leaving now. I will see you later tonight."

"Okay."

"I'll go see if her breakfast has arrived yet," he offers, looking at me. "I am on tonight, so I will see you later."

"He's a nice guy," I say, turning my head in the direction of the door. "He's cute, too," I tease, and Alley smiles. Alison came out as a lesbian almost thirty years ago. But she likes to rate men's looks in terms of whether they are good looking enough to go straight for. As far as I know, there has only been one, and he was a Maasai warrior. She had met him on a three-month camping trip through Kenya.

After working to fail out of the University of Vermont, Alison had convinced our uncle that travel was as educational as going to college. Perhaps, she had told our uncle, travel was *more* important than college. Her ploy worked, and he allowed her to use the money he'd set aside for his younger brother's children's education. And for the first time, she was free of Mother and free of her role in our family, and she was happy.

"I want coffee, I want coffee!" her chant begins again. My world-traveling sister's world has shrunk to this room, her bed, and to diluted coffee and vanilla yogurt.

"Coming right up," I say cheerfully. "Alley, I am just going to mix a little milk in it for you." I keep talking, telling her everything I am doing. "Just testing it to see if it is too hot," I tell her as I take a sip. "Okay." I drag out the word, giving the coffee

35

a higher than just passing grade. Holding the straw to her lips, she struggles to pull the coffee up through the straw. "How are you feeling this morning?" Maybe if she keeps eating, we can go home.

"Okay," she answers, allowing the straw to fall from her lips. She looks up to watch the male nurse return with her breakfast tray.

"My sister thinks you're cute," I tell him as he sets the tray down on the table. I don't know why I am telling him that Alison thinks he is cute—I guess just to hear another voice other than my own.

"Thanks. Alison, I will see you later tonight," he reminds her, raising his voice. "See you later," he says to me, lowering his voice to just below a normal conversational level.

I get to work describing all of Alison's breakfast options in great detail and with enthusiasm. I realize I am talking to my sister as if she is a child. I have never talked to her like that before, not even when she was a toddler.

"I want coffee … I want coffee …" she begins again in a voice deeper and more strained than last night. I tell myself it is because she has been yelling all night.

"I have coffee right here, but first I am going to raise your bed a bit more. I think it will be easier for you."

"Okay."

I hold the cup to her lips and allow her to take a sip.

"So good," she moans.

"Honey, how about a little pudding?"

"Okay," she says. "Vanilla."

"Good choice." I say it as if she has just given the right answer on a television quiz show. I pull the lid off the yogurt.

"Okay, Alley." I stir the yogurt with the plastic spoon, level off a spoonful, and hold it in front of her mouth. I put it in her mouth. "How's that?" I ask her.

"Good. Soooo good!" She drags out the Os in "good," sounding like a television advertisement. In between spoonfuls of yogurt, I take a bite of my eggs and toast.

She is different somehow—different from last night. She has withdrawn from caring about what is happening. There is no Dax or Marco Polo or me. She is now the little curly-haired, blonde baby I'd fed, the two of us alone with our brother in our kitchen with the black Lab hovering patiently nearby, waiting for food to drop.

Lying motionless, with the head of her bed slightly raised, Alison accepts one spoonful after another. She doesn't move her hands or attempt to take the spoon to feed herself. She hasn't asked this morning when we are leaving for Vermont or if I will dye her hair.

"I want coffee," she demands in a strained voice. I hold the cup to her lips, and she pulls on the straw until she is exhausted. By now it has cooled from slightly warm to cold.

"I want it hot. I want it hot!" she orders. I take my hot black coffee, add a little to hers, and hold the straw to her mouth again. She isn't able to pull the liquid up through the straw. I think it is more the smell of the coffee that has her asking for more.

The lights in the hall are now at their brightest, and the foot traffic has picked up.

"Good morning. How are things this morning?" asks the nurse, sticking her head into the room.

"Alley just had some yogurt and coffee." I say this like a proud parent whose baby has just graduated to solid foods.

"Good. How was your night?" She looks directly at me. "You sleep all right?"

"Yeah, just not long enough," I tell her. The nurse gives me a look that says she knows how that feels. "Thanks again for the toothbrush and sheets and blanket."

"You're welcome," she answers. "We are glad you are here." She turns to leave, hesitates, and turns her head. "The respiratory therapist will be in shortly. I'll be back," she promises and then leaves me alone with Alison.

I am waiting for Alley to ask if I have the first-class tickets yet, when we are leaving, and when I will dye her hair. She hasn't asked this morning. Alison is talking very little—not like yesterday, when she was yelling, "Where's my sister?" and then acting so excited to see me.

"Alley, you need anything else?" My sister is staring past me, and I turn and follow her gaze. The television is still on with the volume off. "You want the sound on?" I ask her encouragingly. It is I who needs to hear a voice, even if it is the unexciting, almost-whisper of the golf announcer.

"No."

"Okay," I answer, trying to fake cheerfulness. "Alley, I am just going to clean up this mess from breakfast." I have to stay busy, stay in motion. What is left of her coffee goes into the sink.

The therapist walks in the door as the last of the takeout food containers disappear into the trash. "Good morning, Alison," says the young woman and then looks over at me. She looks as if she could be a high-school student.

"I'm Linda—I am Alison's sister."

"Nice to meet you," she says, giving me just a glance. "Alison, you need to take a few deep breaths." The young woman places the plastic cylinder with the crimped tube in front of my sister. Alison opens her mouth, the young woman slides in the mouthpiece, and Alison inhales. The little Ping-Pong ball barely moves. My fifty-four-year-old sister can't suck in even a shallow breath.

"Alison, a couple more inhales." Alison obediently does it again and again, with the same non-result. Life has been sucked out of her, and there is no more.

"Alison," the therapist says, looking concerned. "I will be back later, and we will do it again, okay?" It isn't really a question. The only questions now are the ones I need to ask the doctor when he arrives.

"No!" cries out Alison, her voice straining in agonizing protest. I turn to see why. The PT from the afternoon before is walking around behind me. I imagine her having just passed the respiratory therapist outside the door in the hall, and the two them rolling their eyes in an unspoken communication of "here we go again."

"No!" cries Alley again.

"Alison." She says the name gently while moving to the side of the bed and lowering the rail. "Alison, we need to get you up and moving." She ignores the pitiful protests of my sister, whose eyes are now so large they take over her whole face. Her black-and-blue hands paw at the bedcovers as her concave cheeks become a watershed of tears.

"Alley, I will be right here," I say softly, wishing we didn't have to frighten her like this. "We will each be on a side, like we did yesterday." My reassurance is of no comfort to her.

"You will drop me!" she cries.

"We won't drop you," I promise. "We will not drop you. Remember when I picked you up when you fell down in your kitchen?"

She nods.

"I didn't drop you then." Those huge eyes are now totally focused on me. "You were so amazed I could pick you up. I didn't drop you then, and there are two of us, and we won't drop you now."

I keep talking, hoping she can just focus on my voice and not on how afraid she is. That's what she did for me when we were up in the airplane with our parachutes on. I was so frightened I couldn't breathe, and she kept making jokes and laughing and reminding me it had been my idea.

"Think about how great you are going to feel after you do this," she had said to me, "and besides, it only lasts a few minutes. Be over before you know it."

"Alison, we won't drop you." As I am talking, the PT is helping her into a sitting position, and we are both inching her closer to the edge of the bed. We carefully slide her legs over the edge of the mattress, dangling, not reaching the floor. They are so thin I think they are going to snap.

"No, no, no …" she sobs. My own eyes fill with tears. Alley is so helpless and scared. I want to rescue her from the therapist, the nurse, the hospital, and mostly from herself.

"Alley, you are doing great," I tell her gently. It is the same voice my sister always used to talk to confused elderly women and animals.

"Alison," says the PT, "good job—you are almost there. I am going to put your slippers on your feet, and then your sister and I are going to help you up and help you walk to the chair." She stands back up from where she'd knelt down in front of Alison to slide her feet into slippers. We each hold Alison on opposite sides, as if we have been doing this together for years, and then begin to lift.

"No. I can't. Please don't do this to me. I can't do this. Please …" Alison cries in her hoarse voice.

"Alley, you don't have to be afraid," I tell her. "We've got you."

"Just a couple of steps and you will be there," the PT says. The cries don't stop, and I want to plead with the PT to just return her to her bed, but I don't. It would mean I have given up on Alison ever getting out of her bed again. It would mean I have given up on getting her on an airplane and taking her back to Vermont, to the medical center, and to her living with me until she is healthy again. It would mean I have given up on my sister.

"Just a little bit farther, Alison," says the younger woman. Alley's body sags, and we both tighten our support. Alley is more frightened this morning than she was yesterday afternoon.

"Okay, Alison, your sister and I are going to turn you, so you can sit in the chair," says the PT. Together, we lift her into the recliner and raise the footrest. In this position, it is impossible for her to fall out. The PT grabs a blanket from the bed and tucks it around her to keep her from getting chilled.

"See, Alley? You did it. You didn't fall."

Alison's eyes move to the television, which is still broadcasting in silence. It has been like this all night.

"Alley, you want me to put on *The Today Show*?" I reach for the remote control and change the channel as I'm asking.

"No," she answers in a voice I interpret to mean that she does not care what I do. I turn it to *The Today Show*.

"No. I don't want to watch it."

I look at her. I wonder why she cares. "You want to watch something else?"

"No."

"Alley, you want me to turn it off?" Alison had always watched the news, *Star Trek*, and our favorite, *Law and Order*. Now she won't watch anything except golf. Two weeks ago, all she wanted to watch was football.

Using the remote attached to her hospital bed, I flip back to the golf channel. Alley seems content to sit wrapped in a blanket, staring at the greens and her new hero, Tiger Woods. He surveys his putt from all angles before standing over his golf ball. He sets his feet and takes the swing.

"I will let her rest for a while," says the PT, "and I'll be back in an hour to get her back into bed." No sooner does she leave when a nurse comes in with clean sheets. Together we strip and remake the mechanical hospital bed. It is only eight thirty in the morning, and already I feel as if I have lived a whole day.

"You want anything?" I ask Alley before I sit down. All mothers know that as soon as they sit, someone wants something.

"Coffee. I want coffee," orders Alley. Her voice sounds more strained and less like her. She does not make eye contact; she just continues to stare at the television, her eyes tracking the golfers walking along the fairway. Her eyes do not follow me as I cross the room and step into the hall in search of the floor kitchenette.

"Can I help you?" asks a nurse, no doubt in response to my puzzled expression.

"I was just looking for the kitchen to get my sister some coffee," I say, giving her my best "I don't want to bother anyone" expression.

"It's against the rules for visitors, but I'd be happy to get it for you," she answers. "How do you take it?"

"It is for my sister, and she needs a lot of milk in it."

"I'll bring two. Be right back."

I walk back into Alley's room, and before I have time to sit, the nurse appears.

"I brought you two cups, a carton of milk, and a vanilla yogurt," she says. "Let me know if you need anything else," she adds cheerfully.

"Thanks so much." I step forward to take the small tray from her. "Thanks again." I turn around to set them down on Alley's table. I take a big gulp of one of them to make room for milk.

"Thanks, Linny," Alley says, taking me by surprise. It has been a while since she has thanked me for anything, but I am more surprised that she has noticed me at all. It doesn't take long for her eyes to fix again on the television, attracted to the movement.

The PT returns, and amid IV tubes and Alley's tearful protests that we will drop her, the two of us half assist and half carry my sister back to her freshly made bed. We make her comfortable with pillows behind her head and under her knees. Her pale, thin arms lie at her sides on top of the blanket. The transitions from bed to chair and back have exhausted her undernourished body.

Standing beside her bed, I study her face. There is a bulge behind her almost transparent lids. The roundness of her face has completely wasted away, leaving sharp angles and dry, thinning hair. I would not recognize her if I casually ran into her on the street.

"You must be the sister from Vermont."

I turn toward the voice and see a tall, lean man about my age, dressed in the long, white medical coat of a doctor, accompanied by a younger woman in street clothes.

"Yes, I am the sister from Vermont," I confess. "My name is Linda Burden." I extend my right hand. The woman introduces herself as the social worker, and we shake hands as well. They both look at Alley. She doesn't open her eyes and shows no sign that she even knows the two of them are in the room.

There is a small stool on casters in the room, and the doctor rolls it around to the side of the bed away from the door and perches on it. The social worker remains standing just behind him. I lower myself to the edge of the recliner my sister has just been sitting in.

"Does my sister have cancer?" The question just escapes my lips; I am usually more polite. I have been waiting for months to know what is wrong with her. The impatience is uncharacteristic, but the stress of not knowing seems to have eroded my manners.

"How long has your sister been living out here?" asks the doctor with a casualness I don't feel.

I draw in a large breath. "About eight years," I answer. I am guessing he is just making small talk before we get to the tough stuff.

"What brought her out here from Vermont?"

"She thought she wanted to work at Best Friends," I tell the doctor.

"Does she drink?" he asks. I look over at Alley. Her eyes are still closed. I want to have this conversation someplace else. I feel funny talking about her drinking with her just feet away. I guess at this point, it doesn't matter if she hears us talking or not. There is little point in not telling him the truth.

"She …" I hesitate. "She has been binge drinking since she was in high school," I answer honestly. I tell him about the time I found her sitting on the ledge of a dorm at UVM with a joint in one hand and a beer in the other. I had to call campus security. I tell him she had been picked up four times for driving under the influence.

"Does she smoke a lot?"

"Yes, a lot, for years—a chain smoker," I reply. "What is wrong with her—does she have cancer?" I ask again.

"Is there a family history of cancer?"

Always with the family history—medical people have no idea how adopted kids hear that question. "My sister and I are both adopted."

"Are the two of you biological sisters?" he asks.

"No, we are not genetically related. I was born in Massachusetts, and she was born in Vermont." I don't know why I added that part. Maybe it makes me feel more real, more normal in an abnormal adoption. We were the very last option to parents who could not move past the loss of their own children.

"Do you know anything about her birth parents?"

"No. I don't have any medical history about either of her birth parents."

"I don't think she has cancer," he says after a long pause, finally getting back to my question. "We have done a CAT scan, and it shows she has the brain of a very old woman. It is smaller, pulled away from the cranium. That is from the alcohol. We are also pretty sure she has had a stroke. We can't be absolutely sure, but chances are she has had at least one stroke … but more likely, she has had several." The doctor stops talking and just looks at me. Whatever questions I was going to ask no longer seem relevant. *My younger sister has the brain of a very old woman*, I repeat in my head. Of course.

"She doesn't belong in a hospital," he continues, filling the silence when I say nothing.

I look back at Alison, with her too-thin body and bruises on her face and up and down her arms. Of course she belongs in a hospital—I don't understand. Where else should she be? I don't say any of this out loud. I give the doctor a questioning look.

"Hospitals are for making people well, and your sister is never going to be well. We can help her to feel better and live longer."

I can hear the unspoken "but" in his tone. "What is really wrong with her?" I want to hear a word like "diabetes" or "cancer"

—something I can recognize, something to blame for my sister's condition. Should I ask for another opinion? But instead I ask, "Can I take her back to Vermont?"

"I don't think she would survive the trip right now." His tone is even and matter-of-fact, and at the same time not unkind.

This is when I realize my being here is not about helping Alley to get better but to help her to die.

"Long years of drinking and smoking and the weight loss have made her very weak. We could arrange to have her moved to a nursing home. There she would get round-the-clock care. They would put in a feeding tube and continue giving her fluids, and she would gain weight. It won't make her healthy, but she will live longer."

"I have promised Alison I would take her back to Vermont … that I won't leave Utah without her." I swallow hard to maintain my responsible older sister role. "Could she go into a nursing home in Kanab, so I can live in her house and take care of her cats and see her every day?" I look from the doctor to the social worker.

The doctor looks at the tall woman. "Call Kanab, and see if they have an empty bed," he instructs the social worker. The stylish woman turns and walks out of the room.

The physician stands up and takes a step toward the rail of Alison's bed. Lifting one of her hands, he slides his thumb over the thin, bruised parchment that once covered a powerful grip.

"She is very sick," he says, not taking his eyes from Alison.

"I understand," is all I can think to say. I do understand. I have been watching my little sister destroy herself for years, especially the last three. It isn't as if I haven't seen her since she had moved to Utah. I have seen her many times. I even moved to northern Arizona and worked on a Native American reservation to be near her. I visited her every other weekend. Each time, she would stagger across the room, screaming at me, accusing me of checking up on her, of trying to change her.

I love her and wanted her to love me, so I didn't confront her. I didn't tell her she had to stop drinking. I had done that each of the four times she had been picked up by the police. I had said that each time she entered rehab. Then, one weekend, when I walked into her house, she said, "You know what I love about you, Linny?"

"What?"

"That you don't try to change me. You love me just the way I am."

I look at the doctor, who is still holding Alison's long, skeletal fingers.

"What …" I try to form the question, to ask, *What do I do now? What do I do to make her better? What do I do with my life without my little sister? What do I do without any link to my childhood? How do I know who I am without my sister, my childhood?* Nothing comes out.

"I am sorry," says the doctor. "She has lost a lot of weight. We will try to place her in Kanab, so you can be near her," he says gently.

"Thank you." It is all I can manage to say right now. All he sees of Alison is what she has done to herself with alcohol and smoking and bad choices.

Still holding Alison's thin, bruised hand in his larger one, the doctor repeats, "We can hydrate her and feed her though a stomach tube. You understand she will never be what we would call healthy. It will only give her more time."

"There are no vacancies in Kanab," reports the social worker, reentering the room. "We can put her on a waiting list, and as soon as there is an available bed, we can move her." The social worker looks expectantly from the doctor to me.

I look up at them both and realize they are both waiting for some sort of response from me. I don't know what to say. I can't make this decision by myself.

"I …" I hesitate. "I … I have to ask Alison what she wants to do." I barely manage to speak above a whisper. Here I am, having this conversation in front of her. She is an adult. She should have some say in what is to happen to her.

I look at my sister. Her eyes are closed, and she has given no sign that she is understanding or even listening to this conversation about how she will never be really healthy again. I don't want to make this decision by myself.

"I will get her file, and we can meet in the sitting area at the end of the hall by the elevators." The social worker's eyes linger on me for a moment before she turns and leaves the room to get Alison's file.

I join the social worker in the large, open space the elevator delivered me to yesterday afternoon. It is a cheerful space gorged with sunlight. The social worker is sitting in a comfortable chair backlit from the large window behind her. A thin file sits unopened on her lap. I pick a chair perpendicular to her.

She watches me as I sit. She looks as if she is working out how to begin the conversation.

"Was Alison ever medicated for obsessive-compulsive disorder?" she asks.

"No," I answer. I am not surprised at the suggestion of OCD, just after three days of observing my sister, that relatively minor issue is what she begins with.

"She should have been. There is no doubt your sister has OCD. Was she ever, perhaps, diagnosed with OCD and not medicated?"

"No, not really … not by a psychiatrist," I said slowly. "We all knew she was obsessive about her house. You know, she was always cleaning. If someone touched something, she was up with the Pledge and a rag." I look past her, out the window. "Mother was always commenting on how messy my house was and how neat and orderly Alison's house was."

"Was your mother OCD?" she asks me.

I had never considered that our mother might have been OCD. "No," I answer. "She was crazy, but not OCD. It doesn't matter anyway, because we were adopted."

"It is interesting that Alison never mentioned being adopted," she says, opening the folder and then looking back up at me.

47

"So you aren't sisters." It isn't really a question—more like she is talking to herself in the same tone one might say, "Isn't that funny?" or "I wonder how that happened."

"In all the ways that are important, we are sisters—we just don't share the same DNA," I say defensively. I am surprised Alley has not said anything about being adopted. It is not like she doesn't remember. It must be on all the intake forms in doctor's offices and hospitals. They give you a list and a clipboard and ask you to check off the medical conditions and diseases a family member may have or had, like in the case of grandparents.

"I am surprised Alley didn't tell anyone here that she is adopted," I say. "Our mother would sometimes introduce us as her adopted children." I want the social worker to know it is a part of our identity. It is who we are.

"Are there any other siblings?"

"We have an older brother. He is also adopted and a recovering alcoholic. He has been sober almost thirty years."

"Was Alison medicated for anything else?"

"She was diagnosed with bipolar disorder and was medicated for that," I tell the social worker.

"So she is medicated for bipolar?"

"No, I think she stopped taking lithium years ago." I try to remember if Alley and I have even talked about what she was taking for medications. I hadn't seen anything is her house, and I don't remember seeing any pills on our trip to Greece.

I try to think of anything that would be helpful for the social worker to know. I could talk about Alison and her life for hours, but I don't think it would be helpful.

"What about your father? You haven't said anything about him."

"He was an alcoholic and a heavy smoker. He smoked four packs a day. He was hit by a car and died when Alison was about twenty. That was about thirty-five years ago."

"Your sister is very ill," she says after a few seconds of silence. Her expression reveals that she is working out how she is going to put the words together to tell me Alison can't survive. "Long years of drinking and smoking, and now the weight loss, have permanently damaged her."

I am silent. What can I say? Do I tell her that all of this is my fault? Do I confess to not taking good care of her?

When I left for college, Alison was beginning eighth grade. I saw her during vacations and on the occasional weekend. When I was in my second year of graduate school, Alley was in her freshman year of college. I was studying psychology to become a school counselor.

I knew how manipulative and destructive Mother had been to the three of us. I knew I had my own problems with depression. I felt so weighed down with the responsibility of rescuing our father, who was a half step away from being a homeless bum; trying to deal with my mother's demands and do something about my brother's drug and alcohol abuse; and separating my own identity from the child I had been adopted to replace. I was so invested in looking together and in control I didn't know that alcohol was taking over my little sister's life.

I told myself she would grow out of it. I told myself each time she came out of rehab that she would get her life together, and for a while, she would. Then our father was hit by a car, and our stepfather got pancreatic cancer. And then I endured a bad marriage and became a single parent to two small children while taking over the day-to-day care of Mother, whose cancer had returned. By the time my daughter went off to college and I had the time and energy to move to the Southwest to fix Alison, it was too late. How do I tell this social worker I waited too long—that I let my little sister down?

"I don't think Alison will agree to go to a nursing home." She only agreed to come here to please me. If only it were possible to turn the clock back.

"Why don't we give your sister the choice of deciding what she would like to do?" suggests the social worker. "I think it is best if the options are given to her by you."

"She will choose to go home." In my head, I am trying to visualize Alley in a nursing home and Alley at home, and what those two options will mean to her and to me. I know she wants to go home. She hasn't asked today when we are leaving for Vermont or if I have the first-class ticket or when I am going to color her hair. Since just last night, she has slipped further from the real world. I don't know if she understands how sick she is. I don't know if she wants to go home to die. "What should I say to her?"

"You can say that she can either go to a nursing home or she can go home." It sounds so simple to hear it from the social worker.

"She will want to go home," I tell her again. "I know Alison would rather go home than go to a nursing home." My eyes fill with tears, and I stop avoiding the unavoidable. *My baby sister is going to die. The doctor said so.*

"Do I have to tell her by myself?" How am I going to tell my sister that if she does not agree to go to a nursing home and be fed through a tube, that her death is inevitable? Never have I felt more alone.

"No, I will be there if you want me to." The social worker's voice is kind.

"Yes."

"I'll meet you in your sister's room when you're ready." She stands up and walks down the hall in the direction of the nurse's station. I am fixed to the chair, unable to move. How am I going to say this? Do I say, "Alley, if you don't go to the nursing home, you are going to starve to death," or do I say, "Alley, what are you thinking? You have to eat!" or "Alley, do you want to die?"

Minutes pass before I finally stand. I look out the window at the city of St. George, Utah. The desert landscape is so far from where Alley and I come from. The colors are so different. I have no friends here, and aside from Alley, I have no other family. My children, back in Vermont, are my whole family. I have to walk back into my sister's room and give her a choice between living a few months longer or going to a nursing home and staying alive for maybe a few more years.

It isn't supposed to be like this. I don't know how it is supposed to be, but not like this. I was planning on taking her back to Vermont, putting her in the hospital in Burlington, and having her live with me.

I look down at the people walking on the sidewalk through the desert garden. They are completely unaware of me standing here, trying to figure out how to offer my sister the choice of life or death. As I watch, I remember the time my uncle called and told me I had to fly to Florida to bring my father home. I was a senior in college at the time, and fishing my drunken father out of the Gulf of Mexico, where he was on vacation on the island of Captive, was not on my list of things to do.

"Why me?" I asked. I had plans, and they didn't include taking care of my father, John. I was staying on campus for the break and teaching skiing lessons at a local ski area.

"Because your brother is too irresponsible, and your sister is too young," was his answer. "You have always been the responsible one."

No one said no to my uncle Ted, and in the end, I went to Captiva Island and dragged my father to the airport. After telling the flight attendants not to give him anything to drink, I took a nap. We had a stop along the way, but we were not changing planes. My father got so drunk the airlines threatened to throw him off the flight.

They had sold the drinks to him, I protested. They let us stay.

After Dad's taxi business had failed, he had done nothing but drink, sleep, and cut the grass. Alison was about four at this time. His older brother by nine years arrived to rescue his younger brother and family. What Dad lacked in self-discipline and drive, Uncle Ted more than made up for. But it was not as easy as setting a model train back on it tracks once it had slipped off. Uncle Ted was accustomed to being in charge, making decisions, and having others do as he instructed. I don't think he understood how much damage had already been done to his younger brother. It was beyond Ted's experience to understand why his brother didn't just pick himself up by his bootstraps and get on with taking care of his family.

At the end of his visit, Uncle Ted settled for making lists of instructions as to what Dad needed to do. He set up college funds for the three of us to get an education and flew back to his home in Marshalltown, Iowa.

Sometime after that, Dad got a job as a professional fund-raiser, working for large hospitals and community funds that kept him away for several months at a time. He now had no parental responsibilities and was free to drink without the nagging. He sent Mother money to run the house and take care of us. She paid the bills and then discovered the checks she had deposited from Dad were worthless. Every time the phone rang must have sent panic through her, wondering if it was a bill collector. I answered a few of those calls and had no idea what the people on the other end were talking about, except they were rude and nasty.

This certainly was not the life my mother had imagined when, at eighteen, she had walked down the aisle to marry the handsome young army officer. Between John's absence and the worthless checks he was sending to her, she was forced to rely on her parents to keep the house and feed her children.

Our older brother would always be too irresponsible, and Alison would always be too young. The role of rescuer had been given to me the day I was adopted. It began with rescuing my parents from the devastation from the death of their daughter and son, and it continued with rescuing my father and caring for my mother.

And now, there is no one else. There are no parents or aunts or uncles to take charge. It seemed to me when I was little that the adults in my life always knew what to do when there was a death or a divorce. Now, I am that adult. How did I get here, to the front of the line? Where have all the years gone?

I turn and walk down the hall. Was it only yesterday when I was greeted by "Where's my sister?" and I hurried to tell her, *Here I am*? Today no one is asking me if I am the sister. The halls are not echoing with Alley's strained voice. There are only the sounds of medical people moving from room to room and the occasional call bell signing someone needing help.

I stop at the nurse's station and make eye contact with the social worker. She stands, walks around the half wall, and follows me into Alley's hospital room.

"Alley," I say softly and touch her arm. "We need to talk." My sister opens her eyes and looks at me with all the trust of a puppy. I can't let her down. I have to do this right. "I flew out here on a one-way ticket, and I will not leave until you are ready to go home with me." I swallow hard in an attempt to prevent the tears threatening to choke me. "I talked to your doctor and to the social worker." I nod in the direction of the tall woman standing just a bit behind me and off to one side. "Alley, we need to make a decision."

"I want to go home." The abruptness of her response to the yet-unasked question pushes me back, and I stand up straight.

"Alley," I begin again, leaning in toward her. "I need to tell you what we talked about."

"I want to go home."

"Alley, you need to hear what the options are." She falls silent, and I mistake this for her willingness to listen to what I have to say. "Honey, you can go to a rehab center—"

"No," she says with all the determination her weakened state allows.

"Alley, please just listen for a minute, and then you can decide. Whatever you decide you want to do is fine. Whatever you decide, I promise I will stay here in Utah with you. I will stay until you are ready to return to Vermont." My sister is silent. "Al, you can go to a rehab center, where there are three shifts a day of people to help you get better, so you have the strength to fly back to Vermont." I pause to let this sink in ... or perhaps just to steady myself to say what I need to say. "They will put in a feeding tube and IV, and—"

"No."

"Alley," I whisper through the escaping tears. I feel the hand of the social worker on my back, steadying me, and I take a deep breath. "Honey, I need you to listen to me, so I know that you understand what your choices are. Alison, I have to know, for myself, that you understand."

"Okay."

"You can go to a nursing home and have the feeding tube and three shifts of professional care, or"—I take a deep breath—"or you can go home and have only me … and I need to sleep occasionally."

"I want to go home."

"Alley, if you want to go home, you can go home."

"I want to go home."

"Al, I need to know you understand. I will stay with you, and I will not leave Utah and go back to Vermont without you." I have to tell her what it means if she doesn't go to the nursing home. I take another breath. "Alley, I need to know you understand what it means if you go home. Al, you need to know that by going home—" The words catch in my throat, and I am not sure I can finish. "Honey, by going home, you will shorten your life."

I said it. I can't keep the tears from falling down my face and splashing down on her clean hospital sheets.

"Linny," whispers my sister, "I did this to myself. I want to go home."

I glance at the social worker. She nods. I don't know if I have done this right. Was there something else I could have said to get her to go to the nursing home?

"I will make the arrangements," says the social worker and then leaves the room.

"Okay, Alley," I tell my little sister. "We will go home."

Physical therapy and the respiratory therapy are halted and a nurse enters Alley's room and removes one of the IVs from her arm. They have left in only the IV to keep her hydrated. I am not ready for the giving up of my sister's life. It feels so final and all hope for her recovery is gone.

Alley is no longer asking for a first-class ticket to Vermont. She is no longer asking me if she will be allowed to smoke in my house or where she will sleep. She is not asking when I will color her hair.

I am not ready.

I'm not ready to lose my sister. This is moving too fast for me. I am going to be alone with her in her house. There will be no nurses or therapists. Alone, I will be watching my sister die. I am not ready. She doesn't understand, does she?

I tell myself that my sister understands her choices and what it means for her to go home. But I don't think Alison really understands she is starving to death. I think she just wants to be in her own house, where she feels safe, and to be with me, with whom she feels loved.

Her lunch tray arrives. She struggles to suck diluted coffee through the straw I hold between my fingers. I spoon-feed her vanilla pudding and yogurt. How good it tastes, she tells me after each bite. This is the most I have seen her eat in months.

"I love you, Linny," she tells me, and I keep wondering how I can live without her.

Alison seems content to stare at the silent television and is now keeping me up-to-date on the comings and goings of Tiger Woods as he strolls the hospital's fairway. *Oh, God*, I think. *Does she understand the choice she has made?*

I look up and see a woman about my age crooking her index finger, indicating that I should follow her into the hall.

"Let's go someplace we can talk," she says. I follow her to the lounge where just a couple of hours ago I sat with the social worker to decide how much longer my sister will live.

She introduces herself as the director of the hospice program and offers me whatever help I think I will need.

Hospice … the end! A tsunami is headed right for me, and instead of running for higher ground, I stand on the beach right in front of it as I watch it advance. There is nothing else I can do. I can't outrun the devastation. And I cry. I cry for Alison, but mostly, I think, I am crying for me. I am so sad; not even during the months of sitting with my dying mother or my stepfather did I feel this alone and abandoned. Maybe it was because I wasn't alone then. I had my sister and my brother, Bob, and my aunt Betty. Now, there is no generation ahead of me to show me how to do this. There is no one here to share the responsibility and to talk me out of my guilt.

I think back to the nights—and there were many—that Alley called me at 2:00 a.m., drunk and yelling at me, telling me how stupid I am. On all the nights she kept me awake, I never yelled at her or hung up the phone on my little sister.

I never told her to stop calling. She would wind down in time, the pain exhausted for that night, and I would be rewarded with her telling me how much she loved me.

Alley and I had been set adrift on a fragile life raft by a mother who could not love us. After the deaths of her natural children, she wouldn't risk that pain again. I fed Alison and took care of her. And then, in her twenties, I detoxed her.

Who else will know about the time she learned to play "Revelry" on a toy trumpet, just so she could stand over my sleeping form at five in the morning to wake me up?

Who will remember all the clear nights Alley and I went outside in all weather, as she pointed to Orion's three belts and the Big Dipper inside of the Great Bear, and my birth sign, the constellation Sagittarius—the archer. Her favorite was Cassiopeia. I think she liked the queen because she liked the way the word "Cassiopeia" sounded when she said it. Alison knew them all. In the summer, we would lie outside on the lawn half the night. I never failed to be amazed at her ability to pick out just the right configuration of stars among the thousands of stars in the sky.

One summer weekend, I was invited to a fiftieth-anniversary party for a friend's parents. I was circulating among the relatives when their striking resemblance stopped me where I stood. I felt my eyes fill and my gut tighten, so I took refuge in my car. I called my sister on my cell phone and told her I was at a friend's family gathering.

"Lonely, isn't it?"

It was all Alison had to say, and I sobbed, knowing she understood the deep isolation I was feeling. Now I was feeling it again.

The hospice director listens without interruption as I highlight our survival. My little sister is dying, and for the first time in our lives, I can't fix it.

I don't think I have ever been so sad. It is a sadness and loneliness that will never go away.

Chapter Four

Alison was really good with animals. After she failed out of the University of Vermont, she appealed to our uncle Ted to let her use the money he set aside for her education to take a trip to Africa. She argued that travel was as educational as sitting in classes. He reluctantly gave in, and she went to Kenya for three months.

When she returned, Alley had no idea what she was going to do with her life. Driving north from our house, she noticed a new brick building going up: a new veterinary hospital. She stopped her car, got out, and walked onto the construction site. There she found the new young vet and asked him for a job.

"I haven't even opened yet," he protested. "My hospital isn't even built yet. I don't have any patience and no money to pay anyone."

Completely unfazed, Alley said with a good-humored laugh, "That's okay—I'll work for free until you make enough money to pay me."

"I don't know how long that will take," the new vet countered.

"It won't take long," said Alison with complete confidence. "I know every dog and cat around here."

She was hired. And she did work for no salary as she helped him build his practice. She worked for him for seventeen years, and then she quit. Alcohol was a major reason for this poor decision.

Alley's resume boasted only a high-school diploma and a failed semester of college. I, Mother, the veterinarian, and some of her friends all pleaded with her not to leave. But she did—whether it was pride, alcohol, rebellion, stubbornness, or because, according to Alison, "I can do better," I don't know.

Several months after she quit, she took a job with another vet. That job ended in days. When I asked her what had happened, she told me he was an idiot who didn't have his office organized right. I was sure she had been fired.

Early on, when Alley was still adorable and kind and working at the first veterinarian hospital, I stopped in one morning. She got there early to walk overnight patients and clean kennels, so I knew she would be there. As I followed her as she went about starting her day, a taxi pulled into the parking area. An older woman got out of the front seat and started to open the back door. Alley must have recognized her, because she greeted her by name, opened the back door for her, and pulled out a carrier. Inside the carrier was a large, fluffy cat.

I held the door open for the owner of the feline and for Alison as she held the carrier out in front of her to fit though the door.

"You are here on the wrong day," Alison told the older woman. "Your appointment is tomorrow morning."

"I am so sorry," apologized the elderly woman with tears in her eyes. "My neighbor was so kind to bring me this morning. I don't know if she can tomorrow."

"No problem," Alley told her. "We will go right in this exam room."

"Alison, I am so sorry. I thought today was the day. I had written it on my calendar." The old woman was now crying at her failure to remember.

Once in the examination room, Alison let the cat out of its crate and began to check the big cat from nose to tail. While she weighed the animal, she alternated between gently reassuring the distraught woman and talking felinese to the patient.

"Good thing you came in this morning. It isn't busy," said Alison, gently coaxing the cat back into the crate.

"I don't know how I am going to get home. I could try calling my daughter to see if she can come before she goes to work."

"No, you are all set—my sister called a taxi for you, and it will be here in a minute. My sister and I will help you."

That was thirty years ago. Back then, Alley had lots of friends, and they had a good time. She shared an apartment with her partner and was learning to take photographs. She was strong. Alison had carried a heavy backpack across Kenya and an eighty-pound pack over the Grand Teton Mountains. Alley had not yet been stopped by the police for drunken driving. She had not yet lost a job because of her drinking.

Two weeks ago when I was with Alison in at her house, she was sitting in her usual place on the couch and I was in mine at the other end.

"I want to watch football," yelled Alison. By then she had already had several punch and vodkas and couldn't walk across the room without stumbling. She had fallen more than once, and that was why I decided to carpet her kitchen and hallway to make them safer. With no fewer than three remote controls in front of her, she scrolled through the channels. It was April, and football was a fall sport, but then, what did I know. It seemed to me that all the sports seasons overlapped.

"Goddamn it," she muttered over and over.

Alison picked up the phone and punched in a number to use speed dial. "I can't find the football game!" she yelled at whoever was unfortunate enough to answer the phone as she accused them of hiding the football game—no "hi," no "good afternoon," no asking about the schedule, just "I can't find the football game!"

"Oh, there isn't one on today? There is no football game on today?" She repeated the question as if the person at the satellite-dish company were stupid. "No football in April? Okay."

Sometimes I hated it when I was right. I pictured the customer-service person turning to a coworker and saying, "You will never believe the call I just got."

She then pulled some papers from the coffee table in front of her and picked up the phone again, the football game completely forgotten.

"I have to renew my car insurance," she told me. She punched in the number.

"Hello?" she said into the phone. "I have to renew my insurance." She paused. "I have to get the number. Just a minute—I have to put my glasses on." She fumbled with her red-framed glasses, undecided whether she should put the phone down and use two hands to get the glasses on. "Lots of people want to buy my car." She read off the number. A brief silence ensued, and I assumed she was listening to someone.

"The phone went dead," she said. "I'll call them back." She redialed the number after a lot of slow-motion shuffling of paper. "Hello? I think there is a problem with the phone. I was calling to renew my insurance, and the phone went dead." She paused. "I have lots of people who want to buy my car. How come the cats can ride for free? Damn ... the line went dead again."

"Let me try," I said, reaching for the cordless phone. I was not sure if she would give it to me or not, but she did.

"Hello, this is Linda Burden, and I am Alison Booth's sister. I just want to check on her car insurance to make sure it is up-to-date." I expected the woman to ask, "What is wrong with your sister? Is she crazy?" but she didn't.

"Her insurance doesn't expire for another six months," the agent answered politely.

"Thank you."

"Have a nice day," she said before hanging up.

"You too," I responded before pushing the end button.

Throughout the years, it was not easy to remains friends with Alison. We would always be sisters, but sometimes that was challenging. After she bought an old house about seven or eight miles from me, I helped her by wallpapering her bedroom, painting the bathroom, and removing a wall to enlarge the living room. For Christmas, I made her a huge quilt. Each square displayed a different endangered species.

The three of us had been raised to distrust one another. When we wanted to talk to one another, we went through Mother. We were rewarded with her attention for ratting out the other two. But going to Mother for help was useless and ultimately dangerous. Mother's need for control and manipulation kept Bob, Alison, and me from creating any sort of relationship with one another. It took courage to go against Mother in defense of a sibling. Alison had a particularly difficult time risking the hurt of rejection.

One late morning, before Alison moved out west, I called and asked her to watch my children for an hour so I could go to a doctor's appointment. She refused. She had no job, she was home alone, and it was only an hour. I pleaded with her, and she still refused. I was hurt.

After she moved to Utah, I was afraid we might lose touch. But the distance made it easier for her to talk on the phone. We talked a lot, usually late at night. And every year, I went to visit her or she came to my house. It was up to me; I would always be the responsible one, and she would always be the little sister.

Last winter, Alley called me late one night and asked if I would take her on a trip.

"Sure," I said. "Where do you want to go?"

"Someplace warm, with a beach. I want to be near the ocean," she requested.

"Anything else? You want it to be on a beach … near the ocean … any other requirements?" I wanted to make sure I could find a place she would really like. I had a time share, so I started searching their properties: Central America, South America, the Caribbean, and then on to Europe. I cast my net further, and a timeshare vacancy on the Greek island of Mykonos came up on my computer screen. I invited my friend K to come with us.

We arranged to break up Alison's trip, knowing that going from the West Coast to Greece would be very hard on her. We met her at Dorval, the airport in Montreal. She emerged from the international arrivals bent over and walking slowly, leaning on a cane. K and I exchanged a look of concern.

Eight months before, when I had last seen her, she had looked thin. I hadn't thought it was possible for her to get any thinner. Seeing her walking toward customs, I didn't know if I could hide my shock at the frail, old woman bent over a cane.

The next morning, we boarded the long flight to Athens. We spent our first two nights in Greece in a youth hostel. The first morning, I insisted we hike up to the top of the Acropolis. Alison didn't want to make the steep climb up the road to the ancient site of the gods. I told her we had all day, and if it was the only thing we did that day, it would be a perfect day. I couldn't let us come this far and not experience the site of the beginning of democracy. I walked up next to her, giving her encouragement and resting with her every few steps.

Once we were at the top, Alison loved it. She loved being there. She couldn't believe she was walking where Pericles had walked. Alley told me the monument had been built to honor the goddess Athena. While at the top, we looked at the statues of the Greek gods and goddesses and the Temple of Athena; we looked down on the Theatre of Dionysus and the city of Athens.

On the way down the paved walking path, I matched my stride to hers. "I'm not having any fun yet," said my little sister. She walked slowly, one foot barely clearing the one in front. Alley leaned heavily on her cane as she made her way down the hill.

"Really?" I had thought she really liked the Acropolis. Puzzled, I asked, "What would it look like if you were having fun?" This trip was about her and for her. I wanted her to have the experience of her life. I would do whatever I needed to do to make sure that when she got home, she would tell everyone she knew that she had had a wonderful time with her sister, Linda, in Greece. I wanted her trip to this warm place near the ocean to be memorable.

"I want to shop," she announced.

"Shop!" I wanted to laugh; this was so unlike Alison. "Okay, we can shop," I assured her.

"Do you know where to shop in Athens?" she wanted to know.

We were walking down from one of the most visited ancient sites in the world. I certainly could take a guess where the shops were.

"Yes. When we get to the bottom, we are going to turn left and walk a couple of blocks."

"Did you read that in a guidebook?" Alley asked. She took my arm for balance to step over a narrow ditch.

I didn't even try to hide a laugh. I looked at Alison in her T-shirt and fanny pack. She looked old in spite of the new running shoes and cargo shorts. I saw the way other visitors looked at her. They saw the walking stick, the stick-thin legs, and the gray skin that was several sizes too big. They must have had the same questions I did.

Sure enough, two blocks farther on were several blocks of gift and jewelry shops promising to give visitors an opportunity to take home a modern replica of the ancient civilization. Alison looked at me admiringly. For once, I felt smart.

In a jewelry shop, Alison found a gold necklace. She had to have it.

"I have always wanted a gold necklace of this design. Linny, I won't use the money we budgeted for the trip." She said it as if she were telling Mother that if she were allowed to go someplace, she wouldn't be any trouble. I felt sad and wanted to hug her.

We had divided the expenses for our trip between us. Alley had sent me half the money, and then I had made the arrangements. The necklace did not fall into the categories of transportation, lodging, or food. I didn't care. If Alison wanted it, that was all that mattered.

"Honey, it doesn't matter. If you want this necklace, then buy it." I was relieved to see Alison looking so excited about something. I guessed she was now having fun.

We waited while the jeweler removed some of the links to make it shorter and then went and had lunch. Alison was wearing the necklace, and she asked both me and K how it looked on her.

"Alley, it is absolutely beautiful," I told my sister.

"It is perfect," K said.

Alison touched it, enjoying the feel of the gold against her pale skin. She looked happy, and we all ordered a different Greek lunch, so we each could have a bite of all three. Alison tried all the dishes.

Early the next morning, we boarded a fast ferry to the island of Mykonos and a slow bus to our hotel. Before we'd left on our trip, my sister had asked me to buy her a portable DVD player—for the plane ride, she had said. After checking into the time share, Alley got out the player and asked me to "make it work."

"I want to watch a movie," she said.

I hooked it up to the television and turned it on. "I just want to watch a movie—you and K do whatever you want," she announced.

We got Alison settled and then went for a walk. K and I passed a motor-scooter rental shop and a restaurant being made ready for the tourist season. A little farther on, we found two fresh markets. We purchased fresh breads, vegetables, and fruits, hoping to encourage Alison to eat healthy.

But she touched very little of those. Instead, she sat on the couch, smoking cigarettes and watching the DVDs she had brought with her.

"She is tired from the trip," I told K. "Tomorrow we will get her out."

The next day, we coaxed her into taking the public bus with us into the port city of Alevkantra, with its narrow streets and blue doors. Using her cane for support, she limped through the uneven streets, which felt more like tiny canyons, closed in by the whitewashed buildings. We explored one passageway and then another. Around each corner was a surprise, and we were never sure we would find our way back.

Alison wanted to buy a watch like mine. It had to be exactly like mine. After searching every shop without success, I unstrapped my own watch and handed it to her. She refused it. Finally, in a small general market, we found a child's watch.

"This is the best I can do," I told Alley. I wrapped the little watch around her wrist. She looked at it a few seconds and nodded that it would do.

The stone streets, hardly more than alleys, were filled with tiny cars and scooters squeezing between walkers and diners sitting in the mid-morning sun at the coffee shops' small, round tables. Mykonians of all ages took no notice of the near misses. They were in no hurry as they sat in front of their homes or walked past clean white staircases and chapels hardly large enough to hold more than ten people.

All of this proved to be too much for Alley's weakened body, and she became agitated and mean. She raised her cane and screamed "Get the hell out of my way" at the local people emerging from their blue, undersized doorways and then disappearing off into the maze of whitewashed homes and shops. I just prayed that any English they might know did not include the words my sister was screaming … although I was sure the meaning was clear.

From under hanging flowers and second- and third-story balconies, we emerged from the maze at the harbor just below four large, perfectly round windmills with conical wooden roofs. The view captivated Alison's photographer's eye, silencing her complaints. The hilliness of the town flattened into the harbor. Boats and ships of all sizes floated in a harbor lined with shops, cafeterias, and patisseries where Greeks and foreigners enjoyed themselves.

The three of us watched a child and pelican approach one another. The little boy gave the big bird a pat on its head in passing. This gave us courage to do the same.

I handed Alison her camera, which I had been carrying in my backpack, and for a short time, she forgot her anger and focused her passion. We were in no hurry; there was nowhere we were expected to be. We followed Alley down the beach as she pursued one shop after another. She was tired; it had been a lot of walking for her. We sat at a table under an awning facing the ocean. No bad views could be found in any direction. A waiter came by, and we each ordered a sandwich. Alison took only a bite or two.

Later that night, Alison complained that the child's watch wasn't right. She wanted my watch with the child's watchband. I swapped the bands and gave her my watch with the child's fake leather band.

The next morning, Alley was still exhausted and wanted to lie in bed and watch television. After cutting up some fruit and making coffee and toast, K and I took a bus to the edge of the city and then another into the interior of the island.

Returning to our hotel, I found Alley sitting outside, under the awning, at the restaurant in front of our time share. On the table in front of her was a carafe of wine and untouched salad. She was pretending to read a paperback book. I sat down at the table opposite her. She didn't greet me or look up. She continued to look from her book to the ocean. The wine glass was mostly full, but the carafe was mostly empty.

"Alley, you want to go for a short walk?" I asked my sister in a soft voice. I felt anxious while I waited to see if she would be pleased I wanted to do something with her. I thought it would be better if she didn't continue to just sit there and drink wine.

"Does it look like I want to go for a fucking walk?" she snarled. She said this without taking her eyes from the gentle waves breaking on the sand just a few feet from where we were sitting. The gentleness of the waves and the harshness of her words left me feeling wounded and confused.

The three vacationers from India we had met the night before walked in, having returned from some expedition. One of them changed course and came to sit with us. I felt relief at the sight of him. He was young and interesting and a distraction from the strain of coaxing a civil word from my sister.

All of a sudden, while I was asking the boy questions about India, Alison struggled to her feet. She picked up her book in one hand and reached for the cane with the other.

"Can't you all leave me the fuck alone?" she barked and then limped away, leaning heavily on her cane.

I was stunned and embarrassed. My chest tightened, and I had the feeling that all the oxygen had been sucked out of the atmosphere. For several seconds, I could say nothing.

"She doesn't feel well," I finally said to explain my sister's rude behavior. I wanted to send her to her room or take away the keys to her car or make her apologize. But she was not a child; she was too old to punish. I told myself it was her behavior that had been rude, not mine. But I felt the guilt by the association of sisterhood.

"She doesn't look well," commented the young man politely. "Has she been ill?" I wanted to tell him how proud his parents must be of him.

Chapter Five: Day Three

I open the front door to Alison's house for the ambulance drivers to bring my sister in. I have shoved a couple of chairs out of the way to give them room to turn the gurney in the living room, giving them a straight path to her bedroom.

"So, you really are a Patriots fan," comments the man in the lead.

"Yeah," Alison answers weakly. It sounds as if they have been discussing football on the two-and-a-half-hour drive from St. George to Kanab.

"Don't think there is enough room to get beside the bed," comments the one who asked her if she was a Patriots fan.

"We will have to leave it here in front of the closet and carry her to the bed," answers the other man.

"Okay."

I had arrived just ahead of them, in Alison's car, giving me enough time to remake her bed with fresh sheets.

"No, you will drop me! No … please … you will drop me!" cries my sister.

"Alison, do you remember how we loaded you onto the stretcher and got you in the ambulance?" The driver was leaning in close, with his hand just barely touching her arm. He lowers his voice almost to a whisper. "We didn't drop you at the hospital and we will not drop you now. We are big guys, and I promise we will not drop you." His voice and tone are gentle and confident, assuring Alison she is safe.

"Okay," Alley says, shedding her resistance. I want to hug this man I have never seen before for his gentleness and tenderness with my precious little sister.

"Okay, Alison, on the count of three," he says. "One, two, three." Using the blanket under her like a hammock, they lift her in unison and place her so lightly and gently on her side of the bed. I can see in their eyes and their sad smiles they know this is Alison's last trip.

The night before, after spoon-feeding my sister her dinner of yogurt, pudding, and diluted coffee, I had lain down on the fold-out couch. The last forty-eight hours had finally crept into my tight, exhausted muscles. It had taken almost a whole day just to get to St. George, and there was no hiding from how very sick Alley was.

My body hurt everywhere. My brain had been in overdrive, first blaming myself for not taking better care of Alley and then making a plan to fix her. It had been my job to take care of her, and obviously I had failed, or we wouldn't be here.

Where could I have interrupted her decline? When she was drinking in the gully behind our old high school? When she was sitting on the ledge of her dormitory drinking a beer? Perhaps when Mother hired a lawyer to keep her out of jail after her fourth DUI? Maybe as far back as when Mother left her for days at a neighbor's house … or when she left her alone with our drunken father? Alley had been little more than a baby then.

"Help me. Help me," cried Alison as soon as I lay down in her hospital room.

"Alley, what do you need?" I asked, getting up from the uncomfortable daybed.

"I need you!" she cried.

"What do you need?"

"Help me! Help me!"

"Alley, do you want the sound on the TV?"

"No," she answered. "Linny, you go to sleep. You are tired." Her voice was suddenly clear and thoughtful.

"Okay, honey. Let me know if you need anything," I told her before returning to the couch.

"Help me! Help me!" Alley cried out again as soon as I committed my back and hips to the foam couch. As she pleaded and begged for help, I got up again and stood, leaning on the rail of her bed. As a child, if I were sick during the night, the only response I got was being told to clean it up. How many times in the last fifty-five years had Alley cried only to have her fears and needs go unanswered? When no one came, had she just given up?

In the hospital I stood at her bedside and offered to get her yogurt or coffee or to change the channel. But she couldn't tell me what she wanted; she didn't know. She apologized for keeping me from sleep.

At about midnight, the same male nurse from the night before came into the room, and Alison cried out, "Help me!"

"Hi, Alison," he said. "Do you remember me from last night? I was your nurse last night, and I am here again tonight. I am going to take good care of you. Do you need anything?"

"No," Alison answered in a thin voice, not taking her wide eyes off him. "My sister is here. She is taking care of me."

I stood beside Alley's bed, resting my hands on the rail, while the nurse took her pulse and made notes on a computer located inside a fold-down desk mounted to the wall next to Alley's bed.

"I'll be back to check on you and to see if you need anything," he told her as he flipped up the portable desk and walked out into the hall.

It had been a long day, and I was mentally and physically exhausted. My legs threatened to fail to hold me up. I had been left on my own to figure out how to rearrange the couch into a bed, so I didn't bother. I lay down on the unmade bed and pulled the blanket up over my head. My body sagged into the cushions.

"I need … I need … I need … help me … help me … help me …" Alley's voice was little and desperate and painful to listen to. It reminded me of when my daughter would cry so hard she couldn't breathe, after her father left. There was nothing I could do to comfort her. Finally, she would exhaust herself and fall into a deep sleep.

"Honey, what do you need?" I tried to keep the irritation out of my voice. Lack of sleep was eroding my self-control.

"What?"

"Alley, you said you need something. What do you need? Do you want something to eat? Do you want coffee?"

"No."

I lay back down and pulled the blanket around me.

"I need … help me … help me … help me …" cried Alison.

I got up and went to her just as the nurse was returning.

"Honey, what do you need?" I asked her again.

"I need … I need …" she repeated just as the nurse came to stand at her bedside opposite me.

How can I take care of her by myself?

"Where is the closest hotel?" I asked, feeling guilty and frustrated and exhausted and close to tears.

"Two blocks west," he told me. "Don't worry, she'll be fine. I will take good care of her."

I just stood by her bed. Tears slid down my cheeks. I felt guilty for wanting to run away. I was so tired. How was I going to take care of her on my own at her house? I stood by her bed and looked down at my dying sister.

"Just go," encouraged the nurse. "Your sister will be fine. It is only two blocks away. I will call you if there is a problem," he assured me as I handed him my cell number.

"Okay, thanks," I said to him. Looking back down at Alison, I said, "Alley, I am going to the motel to sleep tonight."

"Okay, Linny."

I picked up Alison's car key and my day pack and left the room. I almost ran down the hall in my need to escape. I ran from all the little fingers I felt touching me and tugging at my clothes. I felt that if I didn't run fast, whatever was chasing me would consume me, so I ran across the parking lot to Alison's car.

I was abandoning my sister. An audible sob broke free of my control.

At midnight I checked into the same hotel Alison and I had stayed in together when she drove me to the airport. I had no luggage, just a backpack. I tossed the car keys, with their tribal keychain, on the bed and headed for the bathroom. After a shower, I collapsed onto the queen-sized bed and slept.

Now, I follow the gurney back down the narrow hall and out to the front door. I know I don't need to. They would have closed the door behind them. The truth is, I am reluctant to let them go, to be separated from the living. I am afraid to be here alone with Alison. I am worried I won't do this right, I will fail.

I thank them again and very slowly close the door separating me from life. I don't want to watch them back out of the driveway and out of sight. I return to my sister's bedroom.

"Alison, you need anything?" She looks so small in her giant California-king bed. Her black-and-white cat, Dax, leaps up on the bed, landing silently on the opposite corner from her mistress's head. She coils herself into a ball the way my husky does in the snow.

"Linny, can I have a cigarette?"

"You must be kidding!" I blurt out before I can stop myself. What is she thinking? She can't even move her hands, let alone make the ball rise in the tube-thing the respiratory therapist had her sucking on. How is she going to smoke a cigarette? I will have to light it for her. I have never smoked a cigarette in my life. Besides, she has at least one patch on, and I have an entire box of them.

"No," I answer without explanation.

"Shit," she whispers under her breath. "Can I have a beer?"

She is dying as a result of drinking and smoking, and here she is asking for a beer and a cigarette. Is she crazy? I've sat in a lot of AA meetings, and I know the answer: yes. My sister is an addict. My sister is an alcoholic. In a pinch, an addict will drink almost anything that contains alcohol. I once found two large bottles of mouthwash under her bathroom sink. No one buys that much mouthwash unless they are drinking it.

Oh, what the hell. Alley isn't going to get better. The only reason she isn't drinking and smoking right now is that she can't walk to the refrigerator for a beer or muster enough breath to light a cigarette. "Let me see if I can find one." I go into the kitchen and open the right-hand door of her side-by-side refrigerator. I move aside the milk and juice. No beer. Oh, darn, I thought sarcastically.

"Alley, there isn't any beer," I tell her as I reenter her bedroom.

"Can I have a cigarette?"

I walk to the living room and find the pack of cigarettes and a lighter.

"Okay, let me see if I can do this," I say, putting the cigarette between my lips. Jesus, I feel like a middle-school kid. I put my thumb on the little wheel-thing and push down; nothing happens.

If she could do it before she went into the hospital, I should be able to do it. I take the cigarette out of my mouth.

"How the hell do you do this?" I ask Alison. She just watches without answering me. Without the distraction of the cigarette, I keep trying to move the little wheel fast enough to light it. On about the tenth try, it lights. It goes out when I reach for the cigarette. Who would think this would be so complicated? I put it back in my mouth and try again; it lights. I breathe in hard to get it going and immediately begin coughing.

"Why do people do this to themselves?" I ask Alley, not really expecting her to give me an answer. "Here," I tell her, putting it into her mouth. She attempts to inhale, and the cigarette goes out.

"Light it again."

"No."

"Why?"

"Because," I begin angrily, "I have two children, and this isn't how I am going to die." On my last visit, I had spent two weeks in her house, in the room with her, while she smoked one cigarette after another. Sometimes, she had two going at the same time. Alley would forget she had one in the ashtray and take another out of the pack. I watched as she brushed against the one in the ashtray with a careless bump of her hand, sending the first cigarette rolling across the blanket.

"Shit," she whispers.

"How about some yogurt?" I suggest, hoping she will forget about the cigarette.

"Vanilla!" she commands. Good thing I'd stopped at the store on the way back from St. George to buy yogurt and pudding for Alley and rice and vegetables for me.

"Coming right up," I say cheerfully in response to the request for yogurt. I waitressed my way through college and graduate school, so I am familiar with the role of the smiling server.

"This is sooooo fucking good." Alison's eyes are closed, and she looks as if she has just had the best sex of her life.

I am surprised and a little amused by how much she loves vanilla yogurt. She is totally in the moment. After each spoonful, she opens her mouth again like a baby bird. I am the mother, regurgitating food into the waiting mouth of my newly hatched chick. Even back in her own bed, in her own house, she still makes no effort to feed herself or move her hands.

I slide the spoon into the container and fill it again with the creamy vanilla yogurt.

"This is sooo fucking good." She repeats the words as if this is the very first time she has ever had yogurt. She draws out the "so" until it should be its own sentence. Each spoonful of yogurt is honored by the same response until it is gone.

"You want more?" I ask with my feet are pointed toward the kitchen.

"Not now," she says. "I want to get dressed."

"Okay," I say slowly. I am surprised she wants to put real clothes on instead of the hospital gown she is wearing. "You want some warm-ups?" I slide back the doors of the wall-length closet at the foot of her bed. All her shirts are hanging in order according to the length of their sleeves, starting on the left with long sleeves. They are also sorted by color, with the darker ones first. This is broken by a column of cubbies half-filled with neatly folded tees and warm-up pants.

"Which T-shirt do you want?" I ask her.

"I want the one with the blue circle," she mumbles, and I have trouble understanding her.

Blue circle … blue circle, I think. *What is she talking about?* "Alley, what blue circle?"

"You know, the blue circle. I want the blue circle." I cast my eyes up and down and back and forth in her closet, looking for something with a blue circle. I don't see it.

"Be right back," I tell her and walk out of her room into the guest room. I pull out the clothes I left here two weeks before from the drawers and toss them on the bed. *Blue circle … what is she talking about? Damn!* There it is: the blue circle. It is my favorite T-shirt, from the Hopi run I did last year, when I worked on the reservation. On the back is a Hopi runner running through a blue circle.

"Is this the blue circle you want?" I ask my sister, holding it up with the back facing her. She forces her eyes open.

"Blue circle." She looks pleased that I figured it out.

"You want to wear this T-shirt?"

"I want the blue circle."

I untie the hospital gown and slip it down. She makes no move to help me. I slip my own hand through the sleeves and gently pull her hands through. Then I lift it over her head. It feels like dressing my children did when they were infants. I roll her to the side and pull the shirt down in back.

Alison had always been a large-breasted woman and had even considered breast-reduction surgery several times. Two weeks ago, when I helped her in the shower, she had small breasts, and now there is nothing. I can see every bone, every rib in her body. She is so thin I can't imagine a heart, lungs, kidneys, and intestines fitting inside of her.

Alley, what have you done to yourself? I think. She once was so strong and athletic. She wore jeans and T-shirts, for the most part. All efforts by Mother to "dress her up" failed; nothing she said or offered convinced Alison to be the frilly little girl Mother wanted. She would only put on a dress for special events.

"If people don't like me the way I am, too bad," she declared.

Alison had been a solid, chubby baby, and she had never lost the weight. In her teens, she had a great figure. Then, later, she gained about forty pounds. At all these weights, she always had a double chin, round face, and large breasts.

"I'll find you some warm-up pants," I tell her.

"Your blue ones."

"You want my warm-ups—my blue ones?"

"Yes, please."

I go back to the mess on my bed and get my heavy warm-up pants—the ones I wear jogging in the cold desert mornings—along with a ski hat and mittens.

"Here we are," I say, sounding like one of the nurses in the hospital. I pull the sheet and blanket down below her feet to expose bare legs the size of curtain rods covered with bruises that have left her skin discolored and painful looking.

Two weeks ago, Alison could light her own cigarettes and go to the bathroom, hold her own coffee mug, and mix her own drinks. Now she is in adult diapers and literally can't move a finger.

I check her diaper, and she is dry. There is nothing coming out of her! She hasn't peed all day. With all the IV fluids, yogurt, and coffee going into her, why is nothing coming out? I don't understand. I think her body must be holding on to every drop that goes in.

I slip Alley's foot into one scrunched-up pant leg and then the other. I could have fit her entire body into one of my pant legs. It is not that I am fat; she is just that thin. She makes no effort to lift her legs or help me to pull up the sweatpants. She does not lift a finger to do anything for herself.

"Belt," Alison says.

"Okay," I answer. I grab a belt from the closet and start to wrap it around her.

"No, not that one," she corrects me.

"This one?" I ask, holding up another.

"No, other belt," she says.

"This one?"

"No."

"This one?" I ask, holding up the third and fourth and fifth.

"That one." Her eyes fix on her own leather braided one. I poke the non-buckle end under her, reach around, and pull it through the buckle. The belt could easily go around her twice. I cross the ends over her hips and pull the sheet and blanket back up over her.

"Socks."

"Any special ones?" I ask before I gather up every pair in the house and show them all to her.

"Yours."

I go back into my room and pick out the most colorful pair of fleece socks I left here. They look like an assorted pack of Life Savers candy: yellow, orange, and red.

"These okay?"

"Yes."

Pushing the pant legs to her calves, I slowly and carefully slip the socks onto her long, bony feet and then slide the dark-blue pant legs back down over the socks, because everyone likes it that way.

"Can you color my hair now? I want it the same color as yours."

"How about if we do it later?" I suggest. I haven't worked out how I am going to do it. I thought she had forgotten all about it.

"Okay."

"Anything else you want before I take a shower?"

"I want Bun Bun," she demands like a two-year-old.

"What? Who is Bun Bun?" I am at a complete loss.

"Bun Bun," Alley repeats, and her tone says, *Of course you know who Bun Bun is.*

"Just a minute. I will look for Bun Bun." I go in search of anything that looks like a rabbit—I am assuming Bun Bun is a rabbit, anyway. I walk through each room in her house, scanning for something with large ears. I feel tempted to call out "Bun Bun" and see if it comes to me.

I am walking back into Alley's room, defeated, to tell her Bun Bun is nowhere to be found, when I see the rabbits. They sit in plain sight under the drop-leaf table in her bedroom. Bun Bun and the larger bunny are ceramic rabbits. They had belonged to Mother and had been living at my house since her death until about four months ago, when Alison called and asked if she could have them. I wrapped them in bubble wrap and double boxed them and mailed them to her along with a large ceramic cat.

I pick up the smaller of the two and tuck it under her arm. "Here it is. Here is Bun Bun," I tell her tenderly.

"Bun Bun," says Alley. Ceramic is not exactly soft and cuddly, but Alley seems happy to have the bunny on the bed with her.

"Alley, I'm going to take a shower now," I tell her so she will know where I am and that I have not left.

"Okay, whatever you want to do," she tells me. I would normally have worn my Hopi T-shirt, the one I just put on my sister, around the house after a shower, as it is comfortable and my favorite. I find another T-shirt and pair of warm-ups.

"Do you want the TV on?" I ask.

"No."

I leave the pocket door open and turn on the water. I strip off the clothes I have lived in for the past three days and drop them on the floor.

I quickly wash and shampoo, and after rinsing, I punch the shower control in to shut off the water.

"Honey, you okay?" I call out to my sister.

Wrapping one towel around my body, I rub another over my head. I comb my hair out with my fingers and step out into my sister's bedroom. Alley looks restless. Her face is pinched and tight. I pull my tee over my head, pull on blue warm-ups, and lie down on the bed next to her. With my right hand propping up my head, I begin slowly to rub her head. I begin with her forehead and then run my index finger down the bridge of her nose before gently raking through her thinning hair with my fingers.

"That feels so good," she whispers. "Linny, I am so sorry."

My hand pauses for just a second before continuing to stroke her head.

"You don't have to be sorry." I feel my eyes filling, but I don't want to cry—not now.

"I'm sorry. I'm sorry." Tears slide from the corners of my little sister's eyes.

"Alley, it's okay. You don't have to be sorry."

"I'm sorry."

"Honey, what are you sorry about? What do you want to say?"

"I'm sorry."

"Alley, I love you. You are my sister." I begin singing softly and slowly: "Lord help the mister who comes between me and my sister."

Alley smiles. Since the first time we watched the movie *White Christmas*, one of us would say the first line, and the other sister would echo with the second line. "And Lord help the sister who comes between me and my man," I finish. We were Rosemary Clooney and Vera Ellen, and we were going with Bing Crosby and Danny Kaye to Pine Tree, Vermont.

My sister and I hadn't had DNA on our side, so we had forged our bond with iron will and soldered it with love. We reinforced our sister relationship with taking care of one another. Alison gave me humor, and I gave her security. And when our mother locked herself in her bedroom, sometimes for days, we held on tight to one another, telling each other we had not been bad, that we had not done anything wrong. But beneath our brave expressions and talk, we did think we were bad and had done something terribly wrong. Our crime was that we were the wrong kids.

"You want to watch TV?" I ask her, thinking she might want the distraction.

"No," she answers weakly. "Can you color my hair now? Just like yours." I still haven't figured out how I am going to color it with Alison flat in her bed and unable to sit up or support herself. I have been turning the problem over in my head since she first asked.

"How about in a little while?" I ask. "I am a little tired right now. I did buy you a box of hair coloring at the store." I actually bought it two weeks ago to color my own hair. I feel bad putting her off. It is the only thing she is asking for, and I haven't figured out how to do it.

"What color would you like me to color it?" I ask her.

"Blue," she says, and her nod to our old joke takes me by surprise. She has been asking since I got here to color it the same color as mine. In the past, when she asked me to color her hair, I would always ask what color she wanted, and she would always tell me blue.

"Good," I say. "That is the color I bought."

"That feels so good," she tells me again as I continue to rub her head. "Linny, I am sorry."

"You don't have to be sorry," I tell her again.

"I'm sorry. I'm sorry."

"Alley, it's okay. You don't have to be sorry anymore. I forgive you," I tell her. Before we left the hospital, I had called our brother, Bob. I told him she was dying and apologetic.

"Let her apologize," he suggested. "She needs to make amends." I knew this was one of the steps in the AA twelve-step program.

"You want anything?" I ask her now.

"Red Sox hat."

"Okay." I think about her collection of caps.

I roll over in the opposite direction and sit up on the edge of Alley's bed. My feet do not touch the floor, so I push myself off and head for the garage entrance. On the opposite wall from the washer and dryer hang several ball caps. I look them over, bypassing the one from the Utah winter games, two from our trip to Greece, one from Guatemala, a couple of tribal ones, and one from the Andrew Lloyd Webber Broadway show *Evita*.

I find the dark-blue one with a large "B" trimmed in white. I reach up on my toes, push up on the visor, and catch it as it falls. Maybe she has two, so I can wear one, too. Scanning the remaining caps, I don't see one, but I spy one with the same colors. It displays a football player wearing the three-corner American patriot's hat of the New England Patriots. *That will do*, I decide as I tug it down on my head.

I adjust the size of the Red Sox cap as small as I can. Lifting Alley's head slightly, I am able to put the cap on her. She looks so tiny. The cap looks so big. It falls down over her eyes. I push it back up and wedge it against the pillow.

"Looks great!" I make my voice sound as if we have box seats at Fenway. "I have one, too."

She opens her eyes and looks at me wearing the New England Patriots cap as I stand next to her bed.

"Looks good," my sister says and smiles.

"Want me to take your picture?" I ask.

"Yes, please." I get my cell phone from the other room and take her picture.

I lie back down on my back next to her and try to imagine what we look like on this giant bed, dressed in T-shirts, blue warm-up pants, and red and blue ball caps. *Do we look alike?* I wonder. *Can I be both of us? Do I have the strength to transfer some of me into her to make her stronger?* If only I could.

"Linny, we could go on a trip," she suggests, interrupting my thoughts. I need her to live. She is all I have. She is my only connection to our childhood. Who will remember Christmas on Greenbush Road? Who will remember the pond on our stepfather's farm and fishing from the canoe in High Pond? Who will know what only she knows?

"Yep, we could. Where do you want to go?" I ask her as if it is the first time we have played this game. We both know where she wants to go, but we like this game.

"We could go to Africa," she suggests.

"We could, or we could go to Hong Kong. You said you wanted to go to Hong Kong the next time I went." Alison's all-time favorite historic character is Marco Polo. That was why she named her orange cat, a female, Marco Polo.

"We could go to Africa," she suggests like it is a new idea.

"Yep, we could," I say and then pause as if I am considering the idea. "Or we could go to the Galapagos Islands and see those big Galapagos turtles." I took my daughter there before her senior year in high school, and we sent Alley a postcard from the barrel post office.

"Yes, I would like to see the big turtles … or we could go to Africa," Alley says.

"How about Norway? We have never seen fiords before."

"That would be good … or we could go to Africa," Alison suggests.

"Or we could go to Australia," I tell my sister.

"Or we could go to Africa." Her voice is fading, and I sense she is tiring of our game, so I decide to end this game we have been playing for the last five years or so.

"Or we could go to Africa," I concede, and Alley smiles in response. When she was in her early twenties, Alison went to Africa on a NOLS (National Outdoor Leadership School) course. I know it was the happiest she has ever been. She was sober then and didn't smoke.

When Alison returned from Kenya, she gave the family version of her trip, recounting stories about elephants and lions to Mother and our stepfather, Douglas. She told them about climbing Mount Kilimanjaro and the beauty of the plains.

Alone with me, she told me the truth: the real adventure had been falling in love with a Maasai warrior named Booker. A couple of Maasai men had been hired to act as guides. Alison had spent three months hiking and climbing and tenting with Booker. "Linny, I love him," she told me. He would not have been happy living in Vermont, and Alison could not have stayed in Kenya. It is sad to think she had only three months in a life of fifty-five years when she was happy. I would have told her to stay, but it was a different time, with parents of a different generation.

"Linny, would you take me to Africa?" This isn't part of the game. I can't get her to Vermont; how the hell am I going to get her to Africa? I am never going to take her anywhere again. I am never going to ski or play tennis with her again. She will be going nowhere. My eyes fill with tears, and I wait until I am sure my voice will not falter.

"Honey, I will take you to Africa, I promise." I turn my head, and from under the visor of her ball cap, I look at my baby sister. Tears are skiing a zigzag course through the creases in her dry skin. Her eyes are closed.

The phone rings. I roll back off the bed and walk to the kitchen to answer it. It is the local hospice person. She and the nurse want to stop by to drop off some information and a kit and to see what I need.

The two women arrive before I have time to lie back down with Alison and plan our trip to Africa. After introductions, the nurse opens the kit and explains the oral syringes. Some are morphine to be given for pain, and the others, plus some cream, are for anxiety.

"Be sure you wear latex gloves when you apply the cream, or you will be medicating yourself as well," the nurse says. She pulls out some papers. "Also, this is a log to fill in when you give her morphine and the amount."

"How much do I give her?" I ask anxiously. I look up from the chart where I am to fill in dose and time. I hadn't realized I would be giving her medication when we left the hospital. It seems crazy to me now that I hadn't thought about medication. When Mother was bedridden with cancer, I created an elaborate system to keep track of the several pills she was taking. Some had to be given before meals and some with food.

I had help back then. And yesterday, Alley, had three shifts of nursing staff who charted and documented everything.

The enormity of what is ahead is just sinking in. For the next several weeks or months, I am the three shifts a day. I am the record keeper and the cook and the entertainment.

"You just follow the directions," she says, pointing to the columns indicating time and dosage.

What if I make a mistake? What if I can't do this alone? What if I am not perfect? I want to ask her.

"Just follow the directions," she repeats. "You will be fine, and you can call us anytime."

The hospice worker takes a step closer. "Why don't we go meet Alison?"

They follow me down the hall to Alison's bedroom. I go around the bed to my sister. "Alley," I say in a normal tone of voice. Her eyes open, and she looks at me. She doesn't realize there are other people in the room until the hospice worker steps forward and introduces herself.

"Alison, we are from hospice," she says. "We just stopped in to see if there is anything we can do for you." She pauses for a minute to give Alison a chance to respond. When Alison says nothing, she continues, "Alison is there anything you need?"

"I don't need you; I have my sister here to help me," she tells them politely.

"We just want to let you know we are here to help if you need us." The hospice worker is kind to my sister.

The nurse steps around us and approaches Alison. "Alison, can I just look at your hands?" She waits respectfully for Alison to understand and respond.

"Okay."

The nurse gently scoops Alley's hand and cradles it in her own hand to inspect the IV sites and examine the bruises on Alley's hands and arms.

"I like the ink," she comments.

"What?" mumbles Alley.

"The ink—your tattoos. I like them," she explains. Years ago, Alison had a turtle and a lizard tattooed on the back of her arm, just above the wrist.

"Alison, is there anything we can do for you?" the hospice worker asks Alley again.

"My sister is taking care of me." Alison isn't impolite; she just tells them the way it is.

"You have a great sister," the hospice nurse tells Alley.

"I know I have a great sister," Alison says with more feeling than I have seen from her in weeks. "She is going to be a writer someday. I am the main character in her book. It is going to be about me. But it has to be spelled A-l-i-s-o-n, with only one L."

"What do you want me to write about?" I ask her.

"Anything, as long as it is spelled right."

"I know," I say. Alison asked me about three years ago to write a book, and she wanted the main character to be named Alison.

I walk the hospice worker and nurse to the door. After reassurances of offers for "anything you need," they leave.

I take several deep breaths. I am again alone. I am not sure I can do this by myself. I feel like the ground under me is going to give way, and I am going to die with her.

"Alley, you want anything? I ask her, stepping over the threshold into her room.

"Coffee. I want coffee."

"Okay." I walk back down the hall into the kitchen and make a pot of coffee. While I wait for it to finish dripping, I look over the hospice kit. I am almost paralyzed with the responsibility. I don't know if I will be doing this for weeks or months. I reread the directions. I should be giving her some morphine soon.

I put some straws into a heavy beer mug, so I won't have to run back and forth for a straw, grab a vanilla yogurt, and walk back to Alley's room.

"Want some yogurt?" I ask.

"I want coffee."

"It's almost ready," I say. I go back to the kitchen and get the coffee. She isn't able to drink very much of it, just a sip or two.

An hour later, she wants another cup of coffee.

"Okay, coffee," I announce cheerfully.

"Coffee! I want coffee. I want coffee."

I dilute it with milk and, after giving the white-and-blue-striped straw a bend, I hold it to Alley's mouth.

"That is so good," she groans.

"Want more?"

"More," she whispers and takes another sip.

Alison winces; she is in pain. She has never said she hurts or asked for medication. I put down the coffee and tell her I will be right back. I scribble a notation on the log sheet documenting the time and amount of the dosage and carry the syringe back to Alison's room.

"Open your mouth, Alley," I instruct her, and she opens her mouth without question. "I am giving you a little medicine to help you be more comfortable. Want more yogurt?"

"Not right now," she tells me in a tired voice.

The poured remainder of the coffee and milk into the sink becomes a Rorschach test. I watch as it spreads out, changing shape, over the stainless steel before disappearing down the drain.

As I rinse the remains of my own personal psychological test down the drain, I feel out of touch with my children and my friends, but mostly myself.

"I want … I want …" moans Alison.

"Honey, what do you want?" I ask her as I cross the threshold, reentering her room.

"I want … I want …"

"Do you want more coffee?"

"I want … I want …" Her eyes are closed, and the words are like a recording. I don't know if she knows what she wants. I walk around the bed, lie down again beside her, and rub her head.

"Alley, remember the time," I begin, not even knowing if she can hear me or understand what I am saying, "the time when we skied together at Bolton, and from the chairlift, we took turns picking the next trail? And if you picked it, you led the way down, and if I picked it, I led the way down. It was really hard for me to keep up with you. You would always take all the moguls at the top. Damn, that was hard on my knees. Then you would swap gloves with me, because my hands were so cold. Remember that?"

"Cold hands, warm heart," she whispers.

"Well, it was like your tennis game. Your serves made my racquet twist in my hand. Sometimes I just got out of the way, so I wouldn't get hurt." My arm feels numb, and I allow it to fall to the blanket between us. Consciously, I match my breathing to hers. I want to feel what she is feeling. I want to know what she is thinking. She weighs only sixty-three pounds. How long can she survive like this? How long can I survive like this?

"Linny."

"Yeah."

"Linny, I'm sorry."

"Honey, it's okay," I tell my little sister.

"I'm sorry."

"I know you are, Alley."

"I'm sorry."

"I know."

My sister is becoming agitated, and the tips of her fingers are moving as if she is clawing at the blanket. She sobs quietly. I go to the kit and check the log sheet and pick up another needleless syringe of morphine and the anti-anxiety cream. I slip the syringe into the corner of her mouth. With a gloved hand, I rub cream onto both her arms.

Alley's head has fallen a little to her right, turning inside the too-big Red Sox hat. I grab the bill of the cap and give it a little tug to the left to make it straight.

Chapter Six

I had been writing the adventures of Alison and mailing them to her. Then, one night, Alley called after receiving another chapter and said, "Linny, you know I can't read. I'm dys … dys …"

"You mean dyslexic?" I asked.

"Yeah, I'm dyslexic," she confirmed.

"Oh, okay," "I answered, a bit confused. What was she talking about? Alison had read every Stephen King book and bought a set of encyclopedias and read every volume, beginning with A and reading right through to Z.

"It is very short chapter, and you don't have to read it all at one time," I told her.

"I can't read. The letters are all mixed up," she explained. What was she talking about?

My daughter was leaving for college soon. She had been accepted at a university in Washington State. With my daughter away and my son working and living at home, I took a job as a guidance counselor on the Hopi Reservation in northern Arizona. Now with only three hours separating us, I could spend more time with my sister. I drove from Salt Lake City and stopped at Alley's house to spend the night before driving on to the reservation. She was so drunk she couldn't walk across her living room. She weaved and staggered toward me, screaming.

"How dare you show up at my house to spy on me?" she yelled. I was so startled I backed up. "Get out!" she demanded.

"There is no one to tell anymore, Alley. It's just us now," I said. "I am not here to spy or lecture, and I am not mad at you." She stopped short of whatever she intended to do when she saw me come in the door.

"What are you drinking?" I asked. She turned around and looked at the tall glass of red liquid.

"Hawaiian Punch."

"I'll get you some ice and make one for myself," I said.

"Okay," agreed Alley, staggering back to her place on the end of the couch and sitting down. I added ice to Alison's glass, poured myself some Hawaiian Punch, and went and sat down with her.

During the year I spent living in the Southwest, I visited Alison frequently. We spent time taking photos, mostly in her garden. One morning, she agreed to go with me to Zion to take pictures. We stopped at a restaurant for lunch. Alison ordered coffee and a piece of pie. She was quiet—just looked out the window and ate the pie. I paid the bill and got ready to continue our photography trip to Zion.

"Linny, I want to go home," announced Alley.

"You don't want to go to Zion?" I asked. I was puzzled. Going to Zion had been her idea.

"I want to go home." Her expression was flat—neither angry nor sad. Her voice held no emotion; she just repeated her need to go home. We drove home in silence. Once we got into her driveway and parked, Alley got out, walked into her house, and sat down in her place on the end of the couch with a drink. I saw her enough to know she spent her days drinking.

When I left the reservation, I applied for another guidance job closer to Kanab, in Page. If I got the job, I thought, maybe I could live with Alley and commute each day. I paced around her house, waiting to hear back. Whether as a reaction to the idea of having me there all the time or to my anxiety, Alley started yelling at me to get out. I took a walk around the ranchos and thought about where I wanted to live. Did I want to stay out here, away from my friends? In the year I had been out here, Vida, my daughter, had left Washington and was back in Vermont. My son was still taking care of the dogs and the house for me, and I missed Vermont. There was really nothing out here for Alison, either. I knew she loved her house and worked a little in her natural garden, and other than that, she sat and watched television all day and smoked cigarettes and drank Hawaiian Punch laced with vodka.

I walked back to Alley's with a plan: I would move Alison back to Vermont. We had talked about it many times. We had thought about selling both houses and buying another, or buying a duplex, or adding an apartment over my garage.

I added more ice to her glass and sat down on the couch next to her. "Alley, why don't we both go back to Vermont?"

She didn't look at me—didn't take her eyes off the television. She didn't even indicate she had heard anything I had said.

"Alley, what about selling your house and moving in with me … or we can sell both houses?"

"No."

I left later that afternoon and started the long drive back to Vermont and my home. I drove up over the Rocky Mountains and thought about how much Alison would have loved driving across the country with me in the past. Years ago, she would have done it on just a suggestion.

The following summer, Alley came to visit and stayed a couple of weeks. We sat on my deck as she smoked, and we talked about her moving back.

And we talked about Mother.

We never knew what might make Mother angry. One day, a broken dish was ignored, and the next, she would be so mad. It was like walking a tight rope in the dark. We had to be on high alert. A poorly placed foot meant tumbling into the unknown, or off the planet.

The children in my family were property, bought and paid for, and not entitled to separate personhood. Mother had no respect for privacy and would walk into our rooms at any time. It was even difficult to have our own thoughts, and she always assumed we were lying. One day, kids had been smoking on the bus. When I got home, she accused me of smoking. I hadn't and told her so. Mother decided I had, and nothing I could say would get her to stop accusing me. I finally just gave in and said I had smoked.

"I knew it," she yelled. "Don't you lie to me!" She would believe what she wanted to believe. It was about her being right.

This disrespect and lack of boundaries followed us into adulthood. She felt entitled to walk into our homes unannounced. Alison found a solution to Mother's intrusions by drinking and getting a couple of cats. Mother's allergy to the felines kept her visits to Alison's house short.

Alison as a baby.

Alison and Linda with their grandmother, Dede

Alison on her trip to Kenya

Alison and Booker in Kenya

95

Alison entertaining the family at home

Alison wearing our stepfather's hat

Alison and Linda

Alison getting ready to parachute

Linda Burden

Alison at my wedding

Alison and Mother

Alison with my children, Pablo and Vida

Alison and Pablo in the Adirondacks

Dax and Marco Polo, Alison's cats

Indiana Jones the iguana

Alison on our trip to Greece

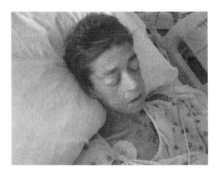

Chapter Seven: Day Four

The chilly air wakes me. I pull on Alison's blue Seattle sweatshirt. She bought it the summer she met my daughter and me in Seattle to look at colleges. Our small world is black and white in the diffused light from the streetlamps. In the kitchen, I fill the coffeemaker from the sink, scoop in the grounds, lean with my back against the stove, and watch the dark liquid drip into the carafe.

I had lain next to Alley all night, and for most of the time, I held her hand. I listened to her inhale slowly, and the hesitation before she slowly exhaled. I held my own breath as I waited between my sister's exhales and inhales, afraid it would be our last together. It wasn't until I heard Alley inhale again that I could stop holding my own breath.

In the darkness, I reach up into the kitchen cabinet above the coffeemaker and take the first mug my hand touches. I fill the mug and without putting on shoes, I silently cross the carpeted living room and escape through the patio door to Alley's backyard. She had bought the two vacant lots on either side of her house and then fenced in the entire property before landscaping it all with native plants, creating an entire habitat.

Alley and I had spent many hours in her backyard taking photographs. She coached me on what would make a good composition.

"Try it from here," she would say, or "let's turn on the sprinkler and shoot though the spray," or "get in closer and see if you can get the bee crawling around inside the flower," or "what about putting Indie"—Alison's pet iguana—"up on a branch in this tree?"

The early morning chilliness of the desert sucks the heat from the coffee. I gulp it down before it becomes completely cold. I want to walk Alley's nature trail she created with colored stones and bordered with larger rocks, but I remain standing on the hard surface of her patio, because I am afraid of what the gravel path will do to my feet.

As if I have my fingers on the sun's rheostat, the light comes up, and I can see the outline of the dark cliffs in front of me. They have endured thousands of years of baking sun, freezing snow, monsoon rains, and winds that drive the sands horizontally through the air, and they will endure many thousands more.

The light has been turned up a bit more, and now the reds and oranges of the sandstone emerge from darkness. The tree in front of me is no longer a silhouette, but a roost for bird feeders and giant wind chimes and the ceramic lizards that my sister loves to tuck in the branches so it looks as if they are waiting to ambush unsuspecting human prey who walk by.

The sun has now climbed over the massive sandstone monuments. Along the house, the snapdragons and butterfly bushes are looking thirsty. The vista is seemingly endless. This is not the landscape of our childhood. It looks more like the moon compared to Vermont's abundance of green and rolling hills and the full and the diverse colors and lakes and rivers.

The sun is above the red cliffs warming the red sand. Alison's rubber gardening clogs are now visible against the side of the house, just outside the sliding door. I easily slip my feet in with room to spare. Climbing the wooden railroad-tie steps, I look around Alley's backyard. Carefully, I set the mug down on the top step, stopping in front of the cedar tree, where the largest of the wind chimes is swaying so slightly it makes no sound. I follow the path as it curves and bends around sweet William, columbine, snapdragons, and blue lobelia. In the fall, Alley had sprinkled assorted seeds to see what would come up.

Circling the birdbath, I skim my fingertips over the cool water. I have done this entire nature walk through Alley's garden many times. It is its own small world, and if I didn't look outside this garden, I would think I were the only person on earth. The garden and house are my sister's entire world and have been for too long.

I have made my way around the entire trail, arriving back in front of the cedar tree, looking down at the terrace. Lowering myself to the top step, I touch the yellow coreopsis growing up between the smooth rocks that decorate the shallow bank on either side of the steps. I pull up my legs and wrap my arms around them against the cold. In another few hours, the sand will absorb the sun's heat, and I will wish for the cooler temperature again.

What little coffee is left in my mug is cold, and I pour it out and watch as it disappears into the moisture-starved ground. Without making a sound, I return to Alison's bedroom and lie down. I pull a blanket over myself and drift into a light sleep.

When I wake up again, the sun is high and shining in the bedroom window. I am tense with indecision. Alley looks so peaceful I don't want to wake her up. I hope with the warmth on her face, she is dreaming of Africa and the Maasai warrior walking beside her. In one hand, he carries a spear, and in the other is Alison's hand. I want to do this right. I want to be a good sister and friend. I want to take good care of her. I want my little sister to know how much she is loved.

I know Alison knows I love her. But I want her to know she is lovable and deserves to be loved. Alison has always believed that if Mother couldn't love her, it meant she was not lovable, that there was a defect in her. She wouldn't believe the defect was not hers, but was Mother's.

"Can you color my hair today?" asks Alley. I didn't realize she was awake, so hearing her voice startles me a little.

"What color would you like me to color it?" I ask, because I always ask her what color when she asks me to color her hair.

"Black, blue, and yellow," she answers.

"Black, blue, and yellow?" I ask quizzically and laugh. "You want any other colors with those?"

"Maybe red," she answers casually.

"Red, too? Have you changed your mind, and you don't want your hair to look like mine?"

"I want my hair to look like yours," she says. "You can do it later—no rush."

"Okay, sounds good to me. Do you want anything to eat or drink?"

"Coffee."

"Be right back." The coffee is all made from earlier this morning, so all I need to do is pour two cups and pop them in the microwave. For Alley, it is milk with a little coffee, and for me, a full mug of black coffee. Grabbing both mugs by the handles with one hand, I pick up a yogurt, a spoon, and a syringe of morphine with the other and carry them back to Alison's bedroom.

I lower the mugs to the bedside table to free up my left hand and then set down the yogurt.

"Honey, I am just going to give you some medicine first," I let her know. I don't want to take her by surprise. But she doesn't seem to want any say in her own care. Not during any of this has she ever asked any questions about her health. Except for when she thinks someone will drop her, I have not seen Alley show any concern. Instead, she opens her mouth obediently, and I slide the syringe between her teeth and push the plunger.

"How about a little yogurt?" I ask.

"Yes, please," she answers politely. She is calm; gone is the venomous anger of two weeks ago. She is as submissive as a lowly member of the wolf pack. She opens her mouth again, and I unhurriedly fill the spoon and guide it in between her dry, cracked lips. I must remember to hunt down some chap stick.

"It is soooo good. It is sooo fucking good," she groans with total satisfaction.

Another spoonful is met with the same obscenity, Alley's highest culinary tribute. "So good. So good," she repeats, as if she has never had anything so good.

"Glad you like it. You want more?"

"Yes, please." Alison says politely.

After taking a swallow of my strong, uncontaminated coffee, I offer her another spoonful and then another until the carton is empty.

"Hello?" calls out an unfamiliar voice from beyond Alley's bedroom. "It's just me," she says.

"We are back here in Alley's room," I call out in response. A tall, slender woman about my own age walks into the room.

"Did you bring me a smoothie?" asks Alison hopefully.

"Yes, I sure did. Would you like it now?"

I hadn't been expecting anyone, except for maybe Alison's friend, LeAnn, and I knew she was working today. The smoothie lady is dressed in shorts and a yellow tank top.

"Hi," I say. "You must be the smoothie lady. I am Linda, Alison's sister."

"Hi, I'm Michelle—or the smoothie lady, as Alison calls me." She holds up the large glass containing the pale red concoction. "Alison has told me a lot about you. She talks about her big sister all the time." Michelle changes her focus from me to Alison. "Alison, I will put the smoothie in the refrigerator for later."

"I want it now."

Like a magician, I hold up a blue-and-white bendable straw snatched from the heavy beer mug on Alley's bedside table that is doing double duty as a straw and spoon holder. I take a step to the side, a movement intended to invite Michelle to take my place beside Alison's bed. She steps into the space, holds the straw firmly in the fruit-colored slush, and inserts the straw into my sister's open mouth.

"Now I know who Alison wanted to call when she was in the hospital," I tell Michelle with a smile. "She wanted to call you from Page to ask you to bring a smoothie. I wouldn't let her call. I didn't know who Alison was talking about or even what. Now I know. Thank you for caring so much for her. It means a lot to Alley. Here, this might work better." I hand Michelle a spoon.

"She could have called me," Michelle says with total sincerity. I wonder if she would have been happy to be woken by Alley from over two hours away just to fulfill a request for a fruit smoothie.

"I just met Alison two weeks ago. I started coming over an hour or two a day and helping Alison with her plants," she says. This explains why I had never met her on any of my visits. Looking back at Alison, she says, "How are you feeling today, Alison?"

Letting the spoon fall from her mouth, Alley says, "okay." Alison is looking very happy with her smoothie and cute in her Red Sox ball cap.

"Good." Michelle looks every inch a gardener with her tan arms and legs. "I am glad to finally meet your sister," she says to Alison.

"She is the best sister in the world," says Alley, her tone carrying a huge amount of pride of ownership. I am the sister—her sister. Her voice is very small; she sounds much more as if she is saying I am the best mommy in the world. Perhaps with enough smoothies and yogurt, Alley will gain enough weight back that she can fly back to Vermont.

"She looks like the best sister in the world," Michelle says with a laugh. Alison is clearly enjoying the attention.

"Alley," I say, "I am going to get you more medicine."

"We will be here," promises Michelle, hinting that she and Alison might just decide to run away together.

When I return, I climb onto the opposite side of Alley's bed, so Michelle doesn't have to move. I slip in the syringe between sips of strawberry smoothie to give Alison another dose of morphine.

Michelle offers Alley another spoonful of fruit smoothie again by holding it to Alison's mouth, but either Alley has forgotten about it or her little body is full. I sit back on my heels and look at Michelle.

"I'll just put this in the refrigerator for later," she offers as she turns to leave the room.

"Michelle, are you going to be here for a few minutes?" I ask her when she returns from the kitchen.

"What do you need?" she asks, giving me her full attention. There is something in her alert and kind face that says she understands the caregiver role and would be happy to help me.

"I just thought if you were going to be here with Alley for a few minutes, I would take a quick shower—if that is okay," I add quickly, not wanting to inconvenience her if she has things to do. The feeling of not wanting to inconvenience her is a holdover from a time when we felt, as kids, that it wasn't okay to ask for anything.

"You go and take a shower," Michelle encouraged. "Alison and I will hang out. Won't we, Alison?" Michelle says this with a smile and a wink at Alley, as if they can't wait for me to leave the room, so they can gossip about my choice of clothes or lack of makeup. I smile at the thought.

"Linny, you do what you need to do," encourages Alley. "Michelle and I will be right here." I catch just a hint of the younger, healthier, funny Alison in her expression.

"Okay, you two, have fun—I will be right back," I promise. "I'll just be right in here." I point at the open door to Alley's bathroom. I feel as if I am leaving my infant with a babysitter for the first time. I don't know why I feel so nervous.

"Okay," they answer in unison, sounding like conspirators.

With clean shorts and a T-shirt under one arm, I slide the pocket door closed. I strip, tossing my clothes on the floor in front of the door, and turn on the water. Standing in the tub, I brace myself against the wall with my hands on either side of the faucets and begin to cry.

Standing up straight, I fill my lungs with the moist air. I feel better after the hot-water massage. With a towel wrapped around me, I stand in front of the mirror and look at my weary face in sepia. I see the mirror image of a mirror image back into infinity. I see our past back to the beginning. If only I could reach into one of the frames and change the course of our lives.

I slide the bathroom door back inside the wall and look at Alison sleeping with her arm still around Bun Bun. Michelle is not in the room. Combing out my short hair with my fingers, I walk down the hall I had carpets installed in two weeks ago and find Michelle sitting on the living room couch with a stack of papers on her lap.

"Linda," she says excitedly, as if we have been friends for years, "I think we can match up these invoices to the items and send some of this stuff back." Alison had ordered the occasional book, CD, or DVD from the Internet, but she had never ordered stuff from the television before.

"What if they won't take it all back?" I ask.

"They have to," Michelle says with confidence. "I was a lawyer in California before my mother and I came to live in Kanab."

"Great. How about you read off the item, and I'll find it?" I suggest. I stand closer to the pile, so I can read the labels. Yesterday, when I walked into Alison's house, I was surprised to see the heap of shipping boxes that easily took up a third of Alley's living room. I stood at the fringe of this pile and looked down, knocking one to the side with my foot. A few of them had been opened, but most were untouched.

Before Mother died, she ordered clothes, bird feeders, Christmas ornaments, kitchen gadgets, and books from catalogs. I think it allowed her to believe she was going to beat the odds. Shopping from the television was Alley's version of ordering from a catalog.

"Standing lamp," says Michelle, reading off the first invoice. I look around the pile; I don't see a standing lamp. "It's over there." Michelle points to the opposite corner. "I think you should keep it," she says. I give her a questioning look. "Alison bought it for you. She said you need it for reading, because you always sit at that end of the couch to read, and there is no lamp at that end."

I look over at the halogen standing lamp. I hadn't seen it yesterday or even this morning. When I was here two weeks ago, Alison had screamed, "Fuck you! Get the hell out of my house." I almost cry remembering how angry Alison was and how hurt I felt … and then she bought me all this stuff. She called me to say she found me a watch with a magnifying crystal, so I could read it without my glasses. When had she bought the lamp—that day, or the next day? I am surprised my sister remembered I had read a book when I sat with her on the couch.

"Okay, what's next?" I ask Michelle in a slow, even tone. I am still thinking about the lamp.

"Running shoes."

Alley can't walk, let alone run. Why would she order running shoes? I find them in the pile and check the size. I want to see if they are her size or mine. They are hers. I put them on top of the invoice.

"Planets."

"Planets!" I look around and spot round spheres about the size of tennis balls on metal stakes. They kind of look like planets. "These, we are going to keep," I say, taking them out in the sun, which is now directly overhead and hot. Holding the tiny Saturn, moon, Mars, and Jupiter one at a time between my legs, I push the metal rods into the hard garden sand. I smile, because these are so Alison. Later, when it gets dark, I will bring in one or two for her to see.

"Blouse and shorts set," Michelle announces.

I spot the clothes lying on top of an open box still in plastic bags. There are two sets; she has ordered each of us an identical set. *Oh, Alley, what have you done?* I shake off the feebleness of my baby sister's efforts to keep us connected. How could she have believed this was necessary?

"Do you want to keep them?" asks Michelle softly.

"No, I would never wear these, and Alley … isn't going to need them." I know now she is never going to get up out of her bed again. She is not going to survive what she has done to herself this time. She has gone too far.

"There are several invoices for frozen and canned specialty foods. I don't know where they are," Michelle says, sounding concerned.

"LeAnn put them in the freezer." LeAnn had called me in Vermont to tell me about the steaks and other frozen foods left out at Alison's front entrance. She said she had stuffed as much as she could in Alison's freezer, and anything that didn't fit, she'd put in her freezer.

With a roll of clear tape from the junk drawer in Alison's kitchen, we finish boxing and labeling the Shopper's Home Network purchases and pile them into Michelle's Jeep Cherokee. I call QVC and explain the situation, and my new friend leaves with my Visa card for the Pack and Ship.

I check on Alison and find she has turned her head and is looking at nothing in particular through the window.

"Linny, can you color my hair now?" she asks.

"Sure." Michelle isn't back yet from mailing the boxes, but I think I have figured out how I am going to color Alley's hair. I go into her bathroom and in the cabinet under the sink I find the hair color I bought for myself a couple of weeks ago. I hold the box in front of Alison, so she can see it. "This is what you are going to look like," I tell Alley. "Are you sure you want it this color?" Maybe she will decide she doesn't want to do this after all.

"I want it the same color as yours," she says, letting me know she is now determined to have dark-brown hair.

"Okay. This is the exact hair color I use on my hair. You hold onto this," I tell her, putting the L'Oréal box under her arm next to Bun Bun. "Be right back. I just need to get a few things from the kitchen."

An idea, or rather a visual, of how to wash and color Alison's hair has been taking shape in my brain. I head for the kitchen, pretty sure how I am going to do this without moving her. I find a saucepan and large plastic cup. Then, I raid her bathroom for all the dry towels in the cupboard next to the bathtub. Stacking these neatly on her bed next to the large saucepan, I look at Alley, waiting patiently with the hair dye tucked under her arm the way she clutched a stuffed rabbit when she was a kid.

"Alley, be right back—just need to get one more thing." I hear the crunch of gravel under tires and know Michelle has just pulled into the driveway.

"Whatever you say," she answers in a monotone voice. Right now, Alley has no choice but to wait for me, and we are both doing the best we can.

"Michelle," I call out, walking into the living room. She isn't there. I step out into the backyard. She has a shovel poised to be driven into the ground with her heel.

"I just thought I would move these. I think …" she begins, but I don't give her a chance to finish explaining her reasoning to move plants around. I don't care.

"Michelle, would you be willing to enter into a conspiracy with me?" I ask.

She looks understandably puzzled. "A conspiracy? Sure, what do you want me to do?" For the first time, I feel as if I will be able to keep at least one promise to my sister.

"Alison has been asking me to dye her hair since I arrived at the hospital. She wants it the same color as mine," I explain to Michelle.

"We are going to color her hair?" She gives me a "you can't be serious" look. I can't blame Michelle; she has only known me for about four hours. "Do you want me to go to the store and buy hair dye?" She says this with a tone of incredulity.

"No, no, that is where the conspiracy comes in. We are going to pretend to color her hair. We are really going to wash her hair. When it is wet, it will look much darker. I just need some help and maybe some garbage bags to put under her, so we don't soak the bed."

"I have a construction bag in my car. I use them for weeding. They're really big," Michelle adds, in case I don't know the size of the bag she is referring to. "Oh, and here is your credit card and receipt." She jams her right hand into her front pocket and pulls out my credit card and several folded receipts. "I'll get the bag."

Michelle goes back out the door we just entered and around the outside of the house to her Jeep. Carrying the folded black plastic, Michelle joins me in the master bath, where I am using the tub faucet to add warm water to the large pan.

"Can you color my hair now?" asks Alison. I am impressed with Alley's single-mindedness about getting her hair colored like mine. She is now wearing all my clothes except for the braided leather belt. And very shortly, with a little luck, her hair will look darker—more like mine—for at least long enough to convince her we colored her hair.

After all these years of telling me how dumb I am for a college graduate she is now wanting to wear my clothes and look like me. She was smart before alcohol robbed her of brain cells. Instead of deliberately failing out of college, she could have graduated. She could have gone on to graduate school or even become a vet. She made nothing easy. I spent my whole life negotiating peace while my sister fanned the flames of confrontation. Her life could have been so different. She didn't have to try to be me.

"Yep, right now," I tell her cheerfully. "I got Michelle to help us." I take the box of hair color out from under her arm, where she had held on to it for me. "Alley, I am going in the bathroom to mix the color."

"It's the same color, right?" she asks, needing confirmation.

"Same exact color," I tell her, holding the box in front of her again so she can see the woman on the cover with dark-brown hair. Peeling back the box top, I pull out the two tubes and larger plastic bottle for mixing.

"Okay." Her voice is now tired.

I go into the bathroom to mix the hair dye, or so I tell her. I mix the liquids in the plastic bottle, but I don't snip off the top.

I am just going to let her see the bottle with the dye all mixed. I will use it later when I color my own hair.

Walking back to the side of Alley's bed, I hold up the bottle in front of her. "Honey, hold this for a minute while we get the plastic and towels under your head." Her hand doesn't move, as I knew it wouldn't. Instead I rest the bottle between her thumb and index finger.

"Okay. I guess we are ready," I say to Alley in a cheerful voice, as if we are off on some great adventure.

Without a word, Michelle and I move like synchronized swimmers as we roll Alley ever so slightly and gently to get the plastic bag and thick towels under her and around her head and shoulders, creating a kind of ditch to catch the water. Next we place doubled-over towels around her upper body to keep her dry. When we are satisfied we have done everything we can to keep her comfortable and dry, I get the pan of water from under the faucet in Alley's tub.

Returning from the bathroom with the plastic cup floating in the warm water, I climb onto her bed from the bathroom side, awkwardly keeping the water from sloshing over the sides. From the pan, I begin ladling small amounts of warm water over Alley's hair.

"That feels so good," Alley coos at our efforts. She closes her eyes and gives herself over to the pleasure of being taken care of by human hands. Michelle and I each rake her hair and massage her head with our fingers.

I catch Michelle's eye and then look at the hair color lying against my sister's hand. Michelle lifts it from where it lies against Alley's fingers.

"Okay, Alison," she begins. "Keep your eyes closed, because we are putting in the color now," she warns as I squeeze a tiny bit of baby shampoo into my hand.

With the gentleness reserved for a newborn baby, I spread the yellow liquid through her curly hair. She moves ever so slightly into my hands, like a cat arching its back. We feel as if we are infusing Alison with love and energy and communicating that anything is possible. She almost purrs with pleasure. Her face is relaxed and content.

Without a discussion of who will do what, Michelle lifts a dry towel from our reserve pile, and I curl up the sides of the construction bag. I carry the black plastic bag, towels, and pan to the washer and dryer. The drenched towels are pushed into the front loader and the bag out onto the garage floor.

"How do I look?" Alley asks, rotating her head just slightly from side to side. Michelle is combing my sister's hair with a wide-toothed comb.

"Honey, you look great," I tell her with a big smile. Her damp hair appears much darker. I get a hand mirror from her bathroom and hold it in front of her so she can see her dark-brown hair—just like mine.

"Alison, you look beautiful—just like your sister," Michelle confirms.

"I know. Linny is beautiful," Alison says with complete sincerity. My little sister's total compliance with and praise of me is a welcome relief and a bit unnerving. I have not always been held in such esteem by my sister.

The sound of the doorbell startles me about an hour after Michelle left to give her ninety-something-year-old mother her dinner. "I'll go see who's there," I tell Alley. A woman I don't know is standing on the other side of the door.

"I am the home-health nurse," she says.

"Hi. I'm Linda—I am Alison's sister," I answer.

"You must be the one from Vermont she talks about—nice to meet you." Seeing my puzzled look at her knowledge of me, she adds, "I was here last week, before she went to the hospital in St. George."

"Oh, okay. Come on in." I step aside, giving her room to enter the narrow hall.

"Let's see how she is doing," she says, turning the corner. She is halfway to Alison's bedroom before I close the door and follow her. "Alison, you remember me? I was here last week. How are you feeling?"

"Fine," answers Alley. "I don't need you. My sister is here taking care of me." Alison is not rude; she is just telling the home-health nurse that her sister will take care of her, and she doesn't need to bother to come anymore.

"Good," the nurse answers. "It is nice to have your sister here to do sister things. I am here to do nurse things. Okay?"

"Okay," concedes the patient, looking neither confused or really comprehending.

"How do I look?" asks Alley, moving her head from side to side. She is showing off her makeover and wants a compliment.

"We colored her hair," I say quickly, needing to protect the lie. I give the nurse a wink and hope she understands enough to just let it go.

"It looks very nice," she responds earnestly.

For the next hour, the nurse examines and records the bruises on Alison's legs and arms. She rolls up my sister's pant legs and peels back her socks. Alley winces and cries out as the adhesive tape is quickly ripped off, but she too weak to offer any real resistance. With the bandages removed, I am seeing these open sores for the first time. The nurse removes a small digital camera from her bag and photographs the discolorations and bruising.

"I am taking pictures, so we will know if they are getting larger," she explains. "The sores are from falling, and given her condition, they can't heal," she tells me.

"Take a picture of my hair," Alley asks before my brain has time to formulate a question. She is feeling so proud with her new clean, colored hair that she wants it documented. And besides, it is proof she looks like her older sister.

The nurse takes a photo of Alley, drops her camera back in her bag, and applies new bandages to just the open sores. Then, together, we slide Alley's socks back on and pull the pant legs down to her feet. It has been a long day.

Alison falls asleep, and I sit in the living room at my usual place on the couch, under the reading lamp she bought for me. Two weeks ago, I would have given anything to have the TV turned off and the cigarettes squashed out. Now I would give anything for Alley to be sitting at the other end with the TV on. The silence is deafening. I look down at the cigarette burns.

She smoked nonstop, all day long, the way our father had. After he had been struck by a car while crossing a main road drunk, Alison and I had to clean out the motel room he had been living in. The bedding, the carpet, and the coffee table all showed evidence of cigarette burns.

How had he managed to avoid burning himself to death? How had Alison kept herself from burning down her house? I had seen her with one cigarette in her hand and another rolling unnoticed across the blanket on her couch. There was always a drink on the table next to her, and the TV was always turned to earsplitting volume.

I have been waiting for the sun to go down and darkness to arrive. As it does, I walk out though the open patio door and climb the railroad ties to the place I had earlier pushed the planets into the ground. The hot, dry earth is giving up its heat to the atmosphere. I look over at Pluto and Saturn and Mars and the moon. I pull the metal rod on which Saturn is attached from the red sand. I carry it to Alison's room. All the little beads inside the tiny globe glow in unison, creating a soft radiance.

"Alley, Alley," I call to her softly to wake her up. "Alley," I say, holding the giant Jovian planet up in front of her. The sphere, having absorbed the sun's energy all day, is now releasing it all into Alison's room.

"Neat," is all she can summon the energy to say.

Chapter Eight

Alley and I took care of our mother for the last two years of her life. She was dying of cancer, a disease she refused to believe she had. She didn't have cancer because, according to Mother, the doctors had never used the "C" word. In all the months she was having radiation and chemotherapy, no one ever said to her, "You have cancer."

For Alley, Mother's illness was my sister's last opportunity to win her love. My sister worked hard cleaning, bringing her meals, changing her bed, doing laundry, and running errands, although Mother knew she had no driver's license.

"Why did she adopt me?" Alley had asked me while sober, while drunk, on the phone, and in person. Alley would ask that same question over and over. She could not bring herself to ask Mother herself, so she asked me.

No matter how much Alley did for Mother, it was impossible to compete with her natural children, who had died before they were five. They hadn't lived long enough to fail a test, track mud through the house, break a favorite dish, or say "I hate you" in the middle of a temper tantrum. They were forever frozen in perfection: adorable and clean and Mother's own biological children.

"Why did she adopt me?" The question just lay there unanswered. While Alley waited on her hand and foot, listening to her talk about how much she missed her biological daughter Heidi, Mother asked Alley to make lunch for my daughter, Vida.

That pushed Alison too far. "You are replacing Heidi with your granddaughter Vida," she accused Mother. "You just want to do it over."

Mother nodded yes. "I want another chance," she confessed. "I have to live to raise Linda's children right." Not only was Mother replacing us by taking my child to give herself a second chance at being a mother, but she had to live to make sure they would survive my bad parenting.

My clever five-year-old daughter figured out that if the mother controls the child, then the grandmother controls the mother. Soon my daughter had my mother reversing my instructions. I finally told my mother she must not interfere with how I raised my children, or the kids and I were leaving.

For the very first time in my life, I had the upper hand and wasn't afraid of Mother. She was, for the most part, bedridden—dependent on someone to feed her, bathe her, and keep track of her medication, and make and deliver food to her bedroom. She didn't want anyone else taking care of her. For her personal care, like helping her in the shower, she wanted one of us. During X-rays, she wanted me in the room to help her maintain a position. The technicians strongly objected, but she insisted, and I stayed.

One afternoon, Mother announced she had hired someone to stay at home with my children, so I could give her my undivided attention. I told her that if I had to choose between my mother and my children, she would lose. She didn't mention it again.

After hearing she was being replaced by her niece, Alison stormed out of Mother's bedroom.

"It's never enough! It's never enough!" Alley screamed. She was right: we were not enough, and no matter how hard we struggled to please Mother, we would never replace the "little sister" and "little brother" who had been victims of Rh+ and Rh– parents. When the mother is Rh- and the father Rh+ the result is mother-fetus incompatibility. The mother's antibodies cross the placenta and destroy the baby's red blood cells. Years ago the second and third pregnancies would result in life threatening conditions. Mother's first pregnancy was a miscarriage. Their next two pregnancies produced a little girl and boy who did not survive.

Mother wasn't trying to hurt her adopted children. She was protecting herself from the pain of ever losing another child. Our parents had been thrilled when they discovered they were having a baby. They learned soon after their daughter was born that she had heart problems—a blue baby. Her blood didn't pick up enough oxygen from her lungs, causing her fingernails and lips to turn blue. It inhibited her activity, keeping her from running or even walking or having playmates. They always knew they could lose her, making them vigilant about meeting all of her needs. Fearing she might not live, they got pregnant again and had a baby boy. He was born with digestive problems and lived less than a year.

Bobby and I had the typical childhood diseases: chicken pox, mumps, and measles. Having a sick child was too reminiscent, too scary for Mother; she would leave the house. Maybe if she couldn't see it, it wasn't happening.

As a small child, I got sick and threw up a lot. Mother would go to her bedroom, and Dad would bring me a glass of water. If it went on for too long, Mother would get angry and yell at me to stop. If it happened during the night, she told me to clean it up. I learned years later in therapy that I had thrown up because of anxiety.

Much later, when I was an adult, I called her from my own house and said I was really sick. I thought she would come get me. Instead, she said, "What the hell do you want me to do about it?" and hung up. I called a friend, who took me to the hospital. I had surgery in the morning.

Death is not the only way a mother can lose a child. As parents, if we do something right, we teach our children to be independent and self-confident. But if Mother couldn't love us, she didn't want anyone loving us. She told the three of us that our aunts and uncles didn't like us because we were adopted. She told our friends that we lied and had mental problems. And this meddling in our relationships was wrapped in love and concern for our welfare. We didn't know our relatives loved us, because we saw little of them and would never have asked. We didn't know she called our friends and asked them not to tell us she called because she was calling because she loved us. Our friends didn't tell us.

It wasn't until I was in my early twenties that I found this out. My friend Pam got a call from my mother with the usual warning not to tell me, but Pam did tell me. "I think you need to know," my friend had said.

Our poor mother was so destroyed by the death of her natural daughter that, with days left to live she wanted to talk about Heidi and how much she has missed her. She describes her sitting in her little rocking chair with her hands over her ears because the vacuum was on.

"How would you feel if Vida died now?" she asked me one night.

Another way she could lose us would be to one another. We could bond and form an alliance with one another against her. She took care of this threat. One of my jobs as a child was to iron my brother's clothes and clean his room. How I resented it! She would tell each of us that we picked fights with the others at holidays, so she couldn't have us all there.

Alison had lost out to the dead children, and now she was losing ground to my daughter. She was hurt by Mother and mad at me, and I am sure she wanted Vida to go away, so she did the only thing she knew to do: Alley went downstairs and had a drink. She couldn't stay sober. She had just returned from a month in rehab after taking a handful of pills and washing them down with vodka winning a trip to the ER and a stomach pumping. When she returned, it was with renewed commitment to taking care of Mother and staying sober—in that order.

"I'm fine. I am never going to drink again," she had told me with complete sincerity.

Having experienced an alcoholic older brother and father, I had heard that before. I wanted to believe her. I needed to believe her. I needed her. "Alley, you know I love you. If you can't take care of Mother and stay sober, don't do it," I told her.

"I want to help," she pleaded. "I can do this and not drink. I will be fine, I promise."

"Alley, Mother is going to die. Right now, you are more important. You have a long life ahead of you. You are more important than Mother. You have to do whatever you have to do to not drink."

"Linny, I won't ever drink again, I promise," Alison said to me.

I knew better, and I still accepted her promise. I needed to believe her. My son was eight and my daughter six; Mother was dying; my husband had left me a month before; and my sister had just gotten out of rehab. But I knew if she stayed with Mother and didn't go to meetings or therapy, she had no chance of staying sober.

We took turns, Alley and me, staying with Mother—Alley during the day and me all night. We overlapped in the afternoon. I watched for signs that Alison was drinking and didn't see any. She was either very clever or I was blinded by my own needs. I also knew my sister needed to feel she was an important part of our mother's care. She wanted Mother to tell her she loved her, and this would be the last chance.

One night, I listened to mother ramble about Heidi and Tommy, her biological children, and how much she missed them. I had heard it all many times. But she seemed to need to talk, so I listened.

"She is drinking again," she mumbled.

"Who?" I asked, knowing damn well who she was talking about.

"Alison. She is drinking."

"I have talked to her about it, and she says she isn't drinking," I said in Alison's defense.

"I can smell it."

"No, she isn't drinking." I knew my mother had an incredible nose and was rarely wrong about these things. *Damn—she promised she wouldn't drink! She promised! How can she do this to me?*

"Pour out all the liquor," she ordered, and I obeyed.

When I opened all those bottles and dumped their contents down the kitchen sink, I knew it wouldn't make any difference. She was an adult now, and Mother's house was not the only source of alcohol.

"What is her problem?" Mother asked. I traced her profile in the muted light from the hall outside her bedroom door. Her eyes were closed, and her hands lay motionless at her sides. If she could have stood and walked to the windows at the opposite wall, she would have seen the moonlight shimmering on Lake Champlain in front of the outline of the Adirondack Mountains. Without getting up and going to the window, I was comforted knowing they had survived for thousands of years.

"What do you mean?" I asked Mother, stalling for time. She could be so cruel.

I was torn about how best I could help Alley. I could run after her to keep her from drinking or having an accident, or I could tell Mother the truth. Was there any point in telling Mother what was going on with her youngest child? It was too late for her to start being a mother now; she was dying, and Alison doesn't need any more shit from her about being fat, or gay, or unemployed. She certainly didn't need Mother berating her about her drinking and certainly not about how disappointing she had been as a daughter. Mother would never understand that none of her living children would ever live up to the imagined potential of her dead children.

"What the hell is the matter with her?" Mother asked again. Her voice was weak, but no less mean.

I weighed my choice of responses. I could continue my assigned role in the family as the peacemaker, the one who smoothes everything over, or for once, I could just tell the truth. I had never done that before. No one wants the truth in an alcoholic family. Our mother had spent her adult life rushing from the pain of her loss and had never stopped protecting herself long enough to let love in or out for her adopted children.

"You wouldn't understand," I finally told her. "What's the point?"

"Try me."

How did I tell my mother that she had been a terrible parent? How did I begin to tell my dying mother that she had neglected her kids? She was so busy falling in love with a married man that she didn't notice her thirteen-year-old was drinking and driving drunk and without a license. Did I tell her that she had never listened, or remind her she had never gone to parent-teacher conferences? Did I remind her that when a teacher called to tell Mother she had concerns about Alison, Mother had told the teacher it was none of her business?

"You have never listened to her," I began cautiously. I paused for a minute, waiting for her to deny my accusation. "You left her at other people's houses, sometimes for days." I was crawling out into a danger zone. "Sometimes she was home alone with Dad, and he would be drunk and passed out. Alison feels alone and lonely and abandoned." Her silence gave me courage to keep going. "She feels you never loved her." Mother said nothing, and her expression was unreadable. "She feels as if you never wanted her, and she doesn't know why you adopted her."

I let us just be in silence, saying nothing, not knowing if she had heard any of what I said. It was Mother who broke the silence.

"You know, when Alison's mother was pregnant with her, she and her boyfriend were found unconscious is a car with the engine running. You think that has anything to do with the way she is?"

"Jesus Christ!" I explode. "You knew that, all this time, and never said anything? You are just wondering now if that might be important for Alley to know?" I wasn't sure if it was important now or not. I wasn't sure if I was angry because she had never thought it might have an impact on my sister's learning or because now I understood that everything she had ever told the three of us about our birth parents was a lie. And years after mother died I learned that Alison's mother had not been found unconscious when she was pregnant with Alison.

I knew the information about Bob and I was all a lie, because in my late twenties, I had driven to Boston and visited the adoption agency that handled my brother's and my adoption, taking my friend Laine for support. There, an experienced social worker with the right combination of toughness and compassion quickly assessed the reasons for my visit. With a large file on her lap, she shared non-identifying information about my birth parents.

"Did you have a happy childhood?" the social worker asked. I then told her about my adopted parents. She opened the file on her lap and read the notes from the time when our parents had first asked to adopt—less than a year after the death of their natural daughter. There were concerns, the social worker read, that the applicants had not done the grief work necessary to adopt a child at this time.

After the deaths of their natural daughter and son our parents pleaded with an adoption agency to allow them to adopt. Reluctantly, the agency allowed them to couple to first adopt a son. The agency felt if they were allowed to adopt a son, the new baby would not be compared to their daughter Heidi, who had died at age four and a half. If all went well, they would be considered for a second adoption, a daughter. I am the daughter who replaced their biological daughter.

"Why did you adopt Alison?" I asked Mother. I want to ask the question for Alison, because she is afraid to ask. She is afraid she won't hear the answer she wants. "Linny," Alley had explained, "I would rather have the fantasy I have created in my head about my birth parents."

But I wanted to know for my sister. Would the truth set her free?

"The adoption agency called," whispered Mother is a weak voice, "and said they had a baby they thought would fit into our family." Mother began hesitantly, clearly experiencing discomfort from her late-stage illness. "We weren't looking for another child." She closed her eyes, and I wondered if she was going to say more. Heidi's death was like a bookmark in mother's life. There was her life before Heidi died and then after her death. Many photos were displayed around the house of the smiling dark-haired child. There were no photos of their son and mother rarely mentioned him, not even in the last weeks before her death.

So, they hadn't really wanted Alison. She was like a door prize. I could think of nothing to say.

"What do you want me to do?" asked Mother after several minutes when neither of us said anything. Her eyes were now open, and she rolled her head to look at me. The cancer had spread into her spine and ribs, so I knew the movement was painful for her.

"Listen to her. Just listen to her," I told her. I was tired, and I didn't want to fight with her. "She needs to talk. She needs to know you love her; she needs to hear you say that you love her." I stood and collected all the dishes and glasses that had accumulated during the day to take them down to the kitchen. "Alley will be back shortly. She is staying with you tonight." She didn't respond. Turning around, I left her room and descended the circular staircase to clean the kitchen and wait for Alison.

It was one of the few nights Alley stayed with her. I was taking my two kids and going home to sleep in our own beds. For almost two years, I had shuttled my son and daughter between my house and my mother's house, because she didn't want strangers taking care of her.

When I got back to Mother's the following afternoon, my sister was in the kitchen.

"I had a talk with Mother last night," Alley said. I felt my body stiffen.

"How did it go?" I asked guardedly. Their so-called talks had never gone over well in the past. But Alley wasn't looking angry or sad.

"She listened to everything I said. She never said I was wrong or crazy or stupid, or that I was imagining things. I feel really good. I feel like for the first time in my life, she really listened to me. Linny, she told me she loves me."

Chapter Nine: Day Five

I lay next to Alley all night stroking her head, holding her hand, listening and talking. I feel that she wants me to stay close.

"Life is unfair," Alley says with a hushed resignation. "I have to clean the house; it must be dirty. The garden needs to be watered and the birdbath cleaned and refilled." Then she cries. It is a very soft, tearless sadness. I tell her I am making sure the house is exactly the way she likes it, and Michelle is watering the garden and keeping the birdbath clean and filled. I don't review and analyze her choices. I just listen.

"Remember how Douglas"—our stepfather—"would give me a dollar for every hour I didn't talk on our nature walks? He said we wouldn't see anything if I was not quiet."

"I remember," I tell her. "We would whisper to you and ask you what time it was, so you would have to talk. You never did, and you always got the dollar."

A couple of times during the night, she asked for vanilla yogurt and ate it with great enthusiasm. And all night, she clung to Bun Bun, the ceramic Dedham bunny.

The early light penetrates the forest green cotton curtains just enough for me to make out the slowly rotating blades of the ceiling fan. I listen to Alison breathing next to me. She takes in a shallow breath and I wait, listening for the exhale. I automatically hold my own breathing to match hers. I do this for three breaths and then gulp in air as if I have been breathing through a cocktail straw. I feel as if I am stealing oxygen from my sister, and I feel guilty.

Of the three of us, why Alison? Why is Alison, the youngest, the one who couldn't get past the neglect? We weren't a real family; we ate no family dinners except at Thanksgiving and Christmas. We stayed in our appointed roles. Bobby was the handsome jock, I was the responsible one, and Alley was the clown. We had to hide Dad's drunkenness and Mother's relationship with Douglas. We couldn't talk about any of the things we were trying so hard to understand. My brother, sister and I looked for relationships away from home. We sat down with our friends for family dinners. We sat on our friends' floors and watched *Looney Tunes* on Saturday mornings.

This morning, Alley is the first to speak. "Linny, I think I can drive you to the airport this morning." Alison has always driven me to the airport in St George. We'd stay in a hotel and have a good dinner at the Outback restaurant. Then, later, we would return to the hotel, and I'd swim in the outdoor pool, and she would sit at a poolside table under an umbrella, smoking a cigarette and keeping me company. The next morning, she would drop me off at the airport and drive back to Kanab.

"Oh, okay. No hurry—whenever you are ready," I tell her without moving. We continue to lie next to one another in silence, just thinking and listening to our own thoughts. Perhaps we are both thinking about what has gotten us to where we are right now. Alison is here because she has been drinking since she was a kid, and I am here because I haven't been drinking since I was a kid. I am here because I love my little sister. I would never forgive myself if Alley died without me taking care of her.

Dax, the black-and-white cat, rises and stretches in the dim light. Without my glasses, I can only see her profile. She looks as if she should be on a broom handle. I reach out to touch her, but she ignores me, and with a light thump on the carpet, she heads silently to the kitchen for breakfast.

I sit up and lower myself to the floor, pulling the cotton blanket off the bed after me. Wrapping it around myself, I follow the feline to the kitchen. I have just passed under a structural crossbeam when Marco Polo ambushes me. She lands next to me on kitchen counter, startling me, before jumping down to the floor. My right hand goes to my chest, where I can feel my heart pounding.

"Damn cat," I mumble to myself.

I open the door to the tall cupboard next to the stove, grabbing a can of cat food. Before I can peel back the lid, Dax rushes to my side. Lifting a spoon from the dish drain, I squat down and shovel some of the wet, smelly stuff into each of the bowls on the floor.

"There. Now behave," I tell the two squabbling siblings. I am a dog person, but I like Dax.

Tossing the empty can and spoon into the sink, I pull the blanket tighter around my body. I rinse out the can and then toss it into the trash. I rinse and clean the spoon and drop the utensil back into the dish drain. I know Alison will never make it out to the kitchen to inspect the damage I am doing to her perfect house, but I know it would upset her if I left dirty dishes in the sink. If Alison feels perfect only when her house is perfect, then I will make it perfect.

Still cocooned in the blanket, I lie back down on Alley's bed and roll to face her. I feel Dax curl into the small of my back, like my husky. It feels good. Dax is the dog of cats. Alison named her after a character from the *Star Trek* series. Dax and Marco Polo were both rescued from the Best Friends shelter as kittens. There is a pet door between the laundry area and the garage. One of the garage windows is left open for them, and they are free to come and go as they please. Alison has always left a window in her Subaru open, and they sometimes sleep on the front seat.

Dax stays close to Alley day and night, just out of striking range of Alison's cane, only leaving her side for kitty-litter breaks.

Except for those outside breaks, the black-and-white cat endures Alley's anger at her declining strength.

The tiniest groan comes from Alison. Wrangling my left hand from my burrito like wrap, I feel Alley's forehead.

"You okay?" I ask, drawing my index finger down her nose.

"Alley?" I pause. "Alley, I'm going to give you some more medicine." I reach across her body and feel for the syringe I left on her bedside table. I used half of it a couple of hours ago. I empty the rest into the side of her mouth and lie back down and stroke her head.

"Linny." Alley's voice is hoarse and tired.

"Al, you want some coffee and yogurt?" I whisper, reflecting the weakness in her voice and the muted light of dawn.

"Coffee and yogurt," she responds, straining her voice.

"I will be right back."

While the coffee drips, I pick up the cats' dishes and put them in the sink to soak, refill their water bowl, and wipe off the place mat laid out as a place setting for Dax and Marco Polo.

Lowering the mugs to the bedside table, I say, "Let's start with the yogurt while the coffee cools a little." I dip the spoon into the smooth, white yogurt and run it around the inside edge, filling it only half full.

"That's so fucking good," she says, dragging out every word—more high praise coming from Alison.

"Glad you like it. How about a little bit more?" I hold a spoonful in front of her, and she opens her mouth.

"That is so fucking good," she says again. I don't know where this "fucking good" description is coming from. I never heard my sister comment on food one way or another before she was in the hospital. I smile.

Alison opens her mouth again, and I guide the spoon in between her teeth. Each taste is as good as the last and gets her highest praise until the carton is empty.

"How about some coffee?" I ask her, putting down the yogurt container and picking up the coffee mug. I bring it to her mouth and watch as she struggles to pull coffee up through the straw.

"So good," she says. I am not sure if she is getting any; it is more the idea of coffee and the smell.

"Let's try the spoon," I suggest. I drop the straw into the trash and gingerly immerse a spoon into Alley's coffee and drip the beverage into her waiting mouth.

"So good," she moans. Alley's thin arms, covered with black and blue splotches, lie unmoving on top of the blanket. "Damn, this is good," she repeats, and I smile at how easy it is to please her.

"Want more?" I ask her.

"Cold."

I warm up her coffee milk by pouring a little of my untouched black coffee into hers. I give it a little stir with the spoon and offer it to her again.

"Good." Her eyes close; it takes energy to keep them open and focused.

"Want more?" I ask.

"More yogurt."

"Alley, you finished the entire carton. You want another one?" I am surprised she is eating so much. Two weeks ago, I begged her to eat. I begged her to drink Ensure and eat the yogurt I had bought. I begged her to have the intravenous fluids at the hospital that her doctor had ordered. She went once and didn't stay.

Every morning, I asked her to go back, and she refused to go. I made her soup and cooked bowls of rice and vegetables, but she wouldn't touch them.

On Easter Sunday morning, Alison and I had gone out for breakfast at a local diner. She ordered fried eggs and toast. She tried to eat the eggs over easy but only managed two or three bites of toast before it came back up into her napkin. But maybe now I can get enough food into her in the next few weeks to get her back to Vermont.

"Alley, I can go get another yogurt." *This is encouraging*, I think.

"Not now."

"A little later," I suggest.

"Later," she parrots back to me.

"Okay. Alley, I am going to take all this stuff back to the kitchen. I'll be right back."

"Okay," she says, as if she is pushing the words through water and it is an effort to get them to the surface. Alley hasn't had anything solid, and she doesn't have the strength to clear her throat.

In the diffuse light from the microwave, I tip the coffee mug slowly and watch as the diluted coffee spills out, spreading out like a river having reached its delta flatlands. It quickly spreads and seeks a lower elevation.

I am left with only the mug. I turn it over in my hand and look at the Native American printed on it. He is holding a lance, a symbol of power and strength. His head is bowed in defeat, the lance all but slipping from his grip. His horse's head is hanging almost to the ground. Their strength is history, their dignity gone; it is the end of their lives as a free and proud people. Of all the mugs my hand touched in the dark, I chose the one labeled "The End of the Trail."

The year I worked on the Hopi reservation in northern Arizona I learned that when members of the Hopi tribe die, they return to the Grand Canyon. Their names are never said aloud again. Saying their names would distract them from their journey to the afterlife.

Where will my little sister go? How can I protect her there? It was not supposed to happen this way. We were to be together to remind each other that Mother's rejection of us was not because there was something wrong with us, but because the good parts of Mother had died with her two natural children. Our trail can't end like this, with her just wasting away. She has to keep eating. She has to want to live.

I finish rinsing Alley's mug and then my own and turn them upside down in the dish drain. I rinse and toss the yogurt containers into the trash. My hand guides the sponge around the sink, across the countertops and stove. I wipe down the front of the refrigerator and microwave. Next I clean the breakfast bar between the kitchen and living room.

I try to look around the room the way I imagine Alley sees her home. The fake sheepskin where Alison sat all day is smoothed out; the ashtrays are all empty and clear; and the shoes are all lined up in front of the stove, with the toes in a straight line just touching the brick hearth. As if I am looking through a wide-angle lens, I inspect the rest of the room and the patio to see that nothing is out of place.

The morning light has now reached into the room, and I run a dust cloth over the coffee table, the end tables and the top of a wooden trunk where Alison stores videos, and the table just inside the door that serves as the depository for loose change and keys. Again, I cast my eyes around the room and allow myself a rare moment of satisfaction. Alison will feel good knowing everything in her house is perfect.

I don't know why it matters now. I don't think Alison cares anymore. She hasn't said anything about her house since this morning, after she said she would drive me to the airport. This hardly seems relevant now. Alley will not walk through and inspect this room again. I want to tell her the house is perfect. Even the carpet looks like a newly mowed putting green.

It never really did matter if Alison's house was clean. Mother would have found something else to criticize. Alley had tried so hard to get Mother's approval, and when she didn't get it, the clean house became a way of controlling something in a world where everything was out of her control.

"Why can't your house be as picked up and as clean as Alison's?" Mother would say once she was inside my door. First, I hadn't known she was going to walk in, and second, I had two small children, two big dogs, and a husband, and I worked. Alison didn't work and had no children; she had nothing else to do. It became something she could best me at, and having a perfect home was what Mother valued. As kids, we weren't even allowed to sit in the living room.

I don't remember the day that Alison decided having a spotless house was something to live for. She'd been a typical kid, flinging her mittens and hats in the direction of the bench just inside the door. It might have been when she moved into our stepfather's house. Her bedroom had been the first in the hall leading to all the other bedrooms. Mother would insist that nothing be out of place, lest Douglas become upset. Alison had no privacy in which to be a teenager.

It wasn't just to me mother sang the praises of another sibling. She did it with all of us. She worked to create a home where her children lived in armed neutrality. The three of us neither, trusted or liked one another. Alison and I struggled to have a relationship, but we were never able to make it work with Bob.

Dax walks past me and down the hall to lie curled up at the far corner of Alison's bed. He never approaches her, and he never leaves, except to eat and to take a quick trip through the cat door to the outside.

Marco Polo, the orange cat, on the other hand, avoids her mistress altogether by disappearing as soon as she is fed and only sneaking back in during the night through an open window to wait out the night sleeping on top of the kitchen cabinets.

I wander back to Alison's side. Her eyes are closed, and she is breathing with effort. I lie down on her bed. I want to be close to her, and I want to be alone, so I leave just a little space between us.

I stare at the slowly rotating ceiling fan. It has a kind of hypnotic effect on me. I roll my head, as Alley did to show off her new hair color, and look over at her. *So why aren't I where she is? How were our lives different?* It isn't the first time I have asked myself that question. When I wasn't asking the question, I had a therapist who did. "Linda, what do you think the difference was growing up for the three of you?"

Lying on my side, I watch the slow, labored rhythm of Alison's breathing. She is sleeping. I can't sleep. Rolling back over to my other side to face the bathroom, I am careful not to disturb Dax. The cat watches me slide off the bed and wander into the next room.

Alley's guest room has always been my room when I am here. The bed, or what is left of it, had been our stepfather's. It once had a yellow silk canopy supported by four tapered posts topped with carved pineapples. The wooden headboard and footboard and the original mattress are all that have survived the thirty-five years since his death. I sat on this bed next to my stepfather and held his hand when he died. I slept in this bed when I visited Alison.

Spread out on the same bedspread, I sat on all those years ago, are my clothes that I scattered looking for the T-shirt with the blue circle. Beside them are my leather journal and a couple of paperback novels. I can hear Mother's voice saying, "You are going to have all this picked up before your husband gets home, aren't you?" It really isn't a question, but a referendum on my housekeeping. I should refold the tees, shorts, underwear, and sweatshirt but I don't feel like it, so I don't.

Turning around, I walk into the smallest of the three bedrooms. Alison had shelves built along one wall, and in the corner is a triangular table made from old barn boards. It is her computer desk. Her laptop remains closed, except when I am here. This room was also once the home of Indiana Jones, the adventurous and monstrous iguana. He lived out the allotted years given to a six-foot lizard of his kind and had simply gone cold, even for a reptile, and died.

Leaning against the door casing, I look at the place in front of the window where Indiana's cage had been. The morning sun warmed his reptilian skin, bringing him to life every morning.

The day he died, I got another one of those late-night phone calls, but this one was different.

"There's been a death in the family," were her first words.

"What?" I jerked myself into a sitting position. I had gone from a deep sleep to a state of panic in five seconds.

"Your nephew died."

"My nephew?" I screamed. I have two nephews; they are my brother's children. *Oh, my God*, I thought.

"Indie died today." Alley's voice was flat and kind of sad.

"Alison, you scared me!" I yelled. It was the adrenalin talking. "What are you going to do with him? Make him into a suitcase or a pair of boots?" *I was cruel*, I think after the words have already traveled through the telephone lines. *No snatching them back now.*

"I thought I'd make him into a belt and keep him around." Damn that girl—always quick with a pun.

"Around your waist? You are really bad," I said.

"Linny, I am really going to miss him."

She had had him for years, so I was sure she would miss that cold-blooded thing. On warm days, all six feet of him swaggered down the hall and climbed the potted ficus tree in the kitchen. When I visited, I insisted the door to this room be closed at night, so I wouldn't run the risk of being ambushed by the dragon on my way to the bathroom.

I step over the threshold of the room, half expecting Indy to skulk out from behind the file cabinet. He isn't here; his cage is gone, not even a hint remains that he lived in Alley's library for several years. The closet doors have been removed, and shelves fill the space from floor to ceiling. Here live the tall books. Books about African art, the human body, and wildlife are all lined up at eye level, along with photo albums from our childhood, her trip to Africa, and her own experiments in photography. I touch the spines of these oversized books affectionately, lingering on a childhood album. I decide I don't want to look at it now. Some of them came from our stepfather's house, a couple were gifts from me, and the rest she acquired on her own. The love of books is something we share.

I leave them and cast my eyes over the shelf-lined wall. Moving in closer, I read the titles, starting with the top left and working my way across and down to the bottom right, like reading a page. She has every Stephen King book ever written and a respectable collection of James Patterson, Michael Crichton, Jean M. Auel, Dean Koontz, Jeffery Deaver, and Native Medicine Wheels. I reach my hand straight in front of me and carefully slide *Cradle and All* from the shelf without pulling the books on either side forward. All the books were perfectly lined up.

I carry the book back into Alley's room and lie down on her bed. Propping the book against my thighs just below eye level, I open the cover, but I make no effort to read. I keep thinking there is something I need to do or have forgotten. I am too tired to think and too restless to sleep. I am not good at doing nothing. I am not good unless I am cleaning or fixing or stacking or reorganizing. Right now I want to fix Alison. I want to load her into her Subaru Forester and drive us back to Vermont.

"Linny, can I have more coffee?" asks Alison. Her transitions from sleeping to waking seem to have become seamless.

"Sure," I say. "Be right back." After rolling off the bed, again being careful not to disturb Dax, I microwave some coffee, dilute it with milk, and grab a yogurt.

"Linny, can I have a cigarette?" asks Alley as I reenter her bedroom.

"No," I answer. Denying her request for a cigarette does not ruffle me. She has a nicotine patch on each arm.

"Shit," she says under her breath like a teenager. I smile to myself. If only someone had told her no forty years ago.

"How about some vanilla yogurt instead?" I offer.

"Yes, please," she answers very politely, as if she is afraid I might be angry about the cigarette. She opens her mouth and waits to be fed. "Thanks, Linny."

"You're welcome."

"Alley, do you want to talk about Mother?" I thought she might have some unfinished sentences, something she wanted to say about the woman who had created so much ambiguity and pain in her life and who had provided the reason for all those late-night telephone calls.

"No," says Alley with no emotion.

When our mother was dying, I would sit up with her sometimes until dawn, just listening. She was the most loquacious during the night.

"I would dream," Mother would say when the rest of the world was asleep, "that I wake up and my mother is standing at the foot of my bed … and I wake up and she isn't there."

"Do you still have the dream?" I asked her.

"No, not for the last four or five years," she answered. I couldn't tell from her expression if that was a relief or she missed the nocturnal visits.

But Alison did not want to talk about her, at least not now. She had withdrawn from the world and for the most part from me as well. Alley had spent so many nights crying uncontrollably. Love and happiness were always beyond her reach. Her birth mother had given her up to a woman who couldn't love, and then Alley had moved on to a series of lesbian partners. Her belief that she was unlovable was self-fulfilling.

"Was I not pretty enough? Wasn't I good enough? Why couldn't she accept that I'm a lesbian?" Alley would always ask so many questions, and I had no answers to give her. And then she would say, "Linny, we really didn't have such a bad life. We got to ski and travel."

"More yogurt?" There is still half left. Earlier, Alley had gobbled down the entire thing.

"No, thank you."

I snap the lid back on the yogurt and return to the kitchen. I have given her more morphine, so I know she will sleep. Taking my time, I put the rest of the yogurt in the refrigerator and rinse the mug. I wonder if I have eaten anything and can't remember. I don't feel hungry, and nothing sounds good. But I know I should eat something, so I settle for some crackers and cheese and then walk back into Alley's room and lay back down on her bed next to her. The sun is no longer shining into her room. Dax is at her post on the far corner of the giant bed. We are like sentries, Dax and me. We are both guarding Alison. I am strangely grateful for the black-and-white cat's company.

Marco Polo's meowing startles me out of my thoughts or dreams—I am not sure which. If I was thinking about something, I can no longer remember what it was. Marco has ventured into enemy territory by crossing over the threshold and jumping onto Alison's bed.

"Okay, okay," I say to Dax, who is now circling me. Exhaustion has made getting off the bed an effort. The cats' mistress's illness should not interfere with their routine. Dax herds me to the kitchen, where I perform the "opening of the cat-food can" ceremony.

Walking back into her room, I find Alley still asleep, the Red Sox ball cap twisted to the right. We would have to have a child's cap for it not to look gigantic on her head. Her mouth has fallen open, and the dramatic thinness of her face is horrifying. It is like an accident you want to look away from and can't.

I want to tell Alley that Mother is not worth wanting to be perfect for and certainly not worth dying for. Not like this. We didn't know until we were adults all the ways Mother had lied to us. How could we? We didn't trust one another enough to talk to one another. If only we had talked.

The sun is sinking over the rooftop. I turn on the shower in Alley's bathroom, leaving the pocket door open in case she wakes up. The hot water feels good, so I just stand under the spray. After dressing in Alley's warm-ups, I push my fingers through my hair and lie back down on the bed next to my sister.

The top of the closet does not go all the way to the ceiling, creating a shelf where Alison displays our stepfather's canoe paddle. It's an oak paddle sanded thin to slice through the water.

"Linny?" Alison says.

"Alley, you need something? You want more yogurt?"

"Linny, if you had been my mother, I wouldn't be here. You would have kicked my ass."

"Yep, I would have kicked your ass," I confirm categorically.

"You are a good mom," she tells me.

"You …" I begin and then lose control and start crying. "You are the only person who has ever told me I am a good mother," I sob.

I roll to face her, and neither of us says anything.

"Linny, can I have more yogurt?"

"Sure, Alley—be right back." I wipe my face with the back of my hand and go to the kitchen.

"That is so good," she moans after the first spoonful.

"Good? Really good?"

"Yep, really good," she says.

"That was so good," Alley announces after the last spoonful of vanilla yogurt. Her words sound as if she is speaking from the bottom of a swimming pool.

"Honey, you want more?" My beer-mug holder is out of teaspoons and I remind myself to bring some back after I toss out the yogurt container.

"Linny, will you take me on a trip?" Alley's eyes are closed, and I imagine she is seeing Booker, young and strong as was more than thirty years ago. "Will you take me on a trip?" she asks again.

"Where would you like to go?" I ask her as if I don't already know. I leave the empty container on her bedside table, walk around her bed, and sit on the bed next to her, leaning up against the wall.

"We could go to Africa," she offers, as if it is a random idea that just came to her.

"Sure, or we could go to Argentina," I counteroffer. I am smiling, because we both know how this is going to end, but we play anyway.

"Or we could go to Africa," she suggests, as if she has not just said Africa.

"Yep … or we could go to Norway," I say casually.

"Or we could go to Africa."

"Or we could go to Hong Kong."

"Or we could go to Africa." Alley's eyes are still closed with the hint of a smile on her too-thin lips. She is totally enjoying this game. It doesn't matter how many times we play it; it is new each time, even if we never change the script.

"Or we could go to Africa," I say, as if it is brand-new idea and she had not just said it.

The hint of a smile on my little sister's lips is now a real smile. "Linny, will you take me to Africa?"

"Sure, I will take you to Africa."

"No, really—will you really take me to Africa?" she wants to know.

"Yes, Alley, I will really take you to Africa," I promise.

"I love you, Linny."

"I know. I love you, too."

"You really are a good mother. Pablo and Vida are really lucky."

"You want to call them up and tell them how lucky they are?"

"Would you give the paddle to Tiger?" asks Alley, pointing with her eyes to the top of the closet. I look up at the canoe paddle. "I think Douglas would like that," she says. Our stepfather loved to play golf.

"Okay," I say, knowing I will never meet Tiger Woods.

"I want to go back."

I don't have to ask Alley where she means. The cotton curtains allow in enough light from the streetlamp for me to follow Alley's profile from the top of her head to her chin.

I know Alison wants to go back to the time before her addiction to alcohol, before she made a habit of being picked up by the police and receiving notifications of court dates. She wants the time before it was necessary to have her stomach pumped of alcohol and pills, the time when she still had a full-time job doing something meaningful that she enjoyed with someone she admired. But the malignancy that started at adoption and fed on neglect and lack of love has gone untreated for too long.

"Linny, will you really take me to Africa?" Alley asks through a pool of phlegm.

I slide my butt forward and lie on my back, staring up at the ceiling. "Yes, I will really take you to Africa."

"Promise you will take me?" she asks again. I don't think she is afraid I won't take her. I think she is afraid she won't be able to go. I imagine she is remembering how happy she had been with her warrior in Kenya.

"Alley, I promise I will take you to Africa," I answer her with total certainty. "We will go to Africa together. We will see elephants and rhinos and lions." I am thinking about her photos. "Vida is in South Africa right now, Alley," I remind her.

"She wrote me a thank-you note."

"Good," I answer. I am glad Vida has developed the habit of writing thank-you notes. When I told Alley that Vida was going to South Africa for two weeks with a college political-science class, Alison had been so excited she sent my daughter $100 to help out. "She sent you a postcard from South Africa. You want to see it?"

"Okay."

I roll off the bed and go the breakfast bar where I have been piling up the mail. I fan it out like a pack of playing cards, pick out Vida's card, and carry it back to show Al. Turning on the light, I hold it in front of her face.

"Can I have more yogurt?" she asks after glancing at the photo of the V and A Waterfront in Cape Town, South Africa.

"Sure. You want me to read the postcard?"

"Okay."

"Hi, Alley,

"Wow, I am in Cape Town right now. Everything is so amazing. Beautiful city—it is very modern! I wish you were here. I've taken lots of photos that I'll send you when I get home. Love you lots, and I hope all is well with you. Love you, Vida."

"Now can I have yogurt?"

"Sure, coming right up." I expected more of a response to hearing from Vida because Alley had been so excited about the trip.

Returning with a half-eaten yogurt and a new fistful of clean spoons, I drop all but one into the mug. "Here you go, Alley." Her eyes close, and her mouth opens.

"That is so damn good. Can I have more?" she asks when the carton is empty. I return to the kitchen and get a full yogurt, and she eats the entire thing.

Turning off the light, I lie back down on the bed next to her. Wearing a latex glove on my left hand, I squeeze a little anti-anxiety cream onto my fingertips and rub it on Alley's arms. I pull off the glove, turning it inside out, and rub her head.

"How does my hair look?" she asks, moving her heads slightly back and forth like a model.

"Looks just like mine," I tell her. She smiles. Dax gets up, comes over, and slinks her body against the back of my thigh.

"Linny, I would do this for you if I could."

"I know you would, Alley. I love you."

Chapter Ten

Beneath the middle-class illusion were bounced checks, wrecked cars, borrowed funds, separate bedrooms, and a failed taxi business our father had run into the ground. Alcohol consumed and destroyed us. It didn't matter that I didn't drink; I hung on to the rim as I watched Alison circle the drain.

Every year, on November 14, the phone would ring late at night. No "hi," "hello," or "how are you," just "Do you know what today is?"

All day, I would not have pondered the date. It always felt like any other day. But, late at night, when the phone rang, I always realized that this day was the anniversary of our stepfather's death. He died November 14, 1978.

"You know what today is?" asked Alison again. Our relationship with Douglas wasn't just about Alison's tennis serve or her commitment to the environment's conservation. A big part of it was the evenings he spent reading aloud to us about trappers, explorers, and captains of industry. He took us on hikes to identify leaves and tree barks and tracks in the mud and snow. Most of all, our stepfather gave us a reprieve from Mother's criticism. This was not thought out or intentional on his part; he just loved to teach. Mother was so occupied with Douglas she had little energy left to wonder what we were up to, least of all Alison.

Alison reveled in Mother's inability to know what her youngest child was up to. Alley came and went from home as she pleased. As long as Alison did not create any embarrassment for Mother or cause Douglas any disruption to his customary well-ordered household, all was well. Besides, we all knew that if she had to choose between her husband and her children, she would choose her husband. We knew this because she told us.

Douglas was the only person Mother allowed herself to love after the death of her children. Our stepfather was unaware of the barrier his wife created between herself and her three adopted children or the one she created between each of the children.

His value as a stepfather was not limited to monopolizing his wife's time. He made the woodmen and explorers in the books he read come alive. We could feel the chill of the snow making its way through our outer clothes high in the Himalayas. We followed the paw prints of the largest tiger into the jungle, and we looked to the Canadian wilderness with our stepfather as our guide. And we loved him.

With dinner we got a banquet size helping of geography. We were quizzed on the locations of the world's rivers, mountain ranges, oceans, countries, and natural resources.

Massive photo albums depicting his travels filled an entire shelf in the living room. For Alley and me, it was an invitation. He inspired our dream to see the world. At twenty-three, I went alone to Japan and visited many of the same places he had gone decades and two world wars before. Old people honored me as the daughter of someone who had known them before they attacked Pearl Harbor and we dropped a bomb on Hiroshima.

Alison read the travels of Marco Polo and dreamed of following in his footsteps. Whether it was to see the world Douglas read about or to concoct stories of our own adventures or to be outside Mother's influence, we both yearned to travel.

Until Mother was in her late sixties and went to Florida, she had only twice before traveled beyond New England and never outside the country. Her world was small; it rarely expanded beyond their property. In this world in miniature, Mother was the monarch. As self-appointed ruler, she could only oversee her tiny kingdom. Her goal was not so much to dominate but to protect herself from any more loss. Loss, however, was to find her holed up inside her well-fortified wall in the form of pancreatic cancer. Her husband was diagnosed at the age of eighty. He was otherwise a healthy active man who took daily walks, read endlessly, and wrote letters to the editor on a variety of subjects.

When Douglas first went into the hospital, she spent every minute at his bedside. After determining there was nothing else the doctors could do for him, he went home. It was a warm fall, and he spent a lot of time sitting outside in the sun, wrapped in a blanket. He still ate, but in small amounts, and he stopped writing letters to the newspaper. The outside world began to matter less. The signs that she was going to lose him, someone she loved, could no longer be ignored. She did the only thing she could do: she pretended it was not happening. She locked herself in her bedroom.

Our stepfather's illness happened at the same time our father had a stroke and then a heart attack. I'd been working in Massachusetts at the time. I resigned from my job and returned to Vermont to help. I easily got another job just beyond mother's fiefdom and lived in a section of my stepfather's house.

After getting home from the hospital in the afternoon, Douglas complained that he had not had anything to eat all day, and Mother was locked in her bedroom and would not open the door. I fed him and assured him his wife would be fine. It was not my first experience with her locking herself in her room. Mother's self-imposed imprisonment lasted for several days. His wife's withdrawal from him when he really needed her left Douglas distressed and frightened. He didn't know if he should go stay with one of his children. He looked lost and hurt. Eventually Mother came of her room as if nothing about her behavior were odd. She sat with him, offering him food, reading to him, and holding his hand.

Alley's late-night telephone call was not to remind me of the date of Douglas's death, but to irrigate memories with the flow of stories to bring him back to life. His predictability had given us security. We knew where he was and that he felt passionate about protecting the environment and supporting free enterprise.

It wasn't for Mother's sake that we behaved; it was for ourselves. We enjoyed the stories, and he enjoyed the audience. It mattered to us what he thought of us. We knew what he valued, and we worked hard to develop those things within ourselves. Alley became an excellent skier and tennis player, and I became a reader of the articles he found interesting.

But it wasn't all perfect. Our stepfather was a believer that DNA makes each of us who we are. He couldn't make the connection between our being adopted and how this information might make us feel. He was so committed to this belief in genetics that once I became a teenager, I was required to spend every weekend at our stepfather's farm. My birth mother had gotten pregnant as a teenager, and therefore they were afraid I would as well. It wasn't that I didn't love it there; I did. But I also wanted to go to school dances, ski with the ski team, and be with my friends. I resented Mother and Douglas thinking I would get pregnant because it was programmed into my genetic code.

After I went away to college, I began to find my own articles offering arguments against the ones he was mailing to me. I had a history professor who told me my reasoning was sound, but I would lose if I didn't get off my soapbox. I learned to use a dispassionate approach in presenting the other side.

This father figure, whom I loved, found my independence disturbing. As a child, I had sat quietly, listening to and believing every word. Now, I was challenging his ideas about race, intelligence, economics, and the Vietnam War. I was too young to take into account his experiences and background and how traitorous my coming of age must have felt to him. He was fifty years older than I was.

Alison wasn't interested in reading articles about genetics or the war. She was just entering high school and was living in a house with an unattended open bar in the corner of the living room. As a small child, she had been left alone with a father who never drew a sober breath. She knew her way around a bar, and she was already a dry martini expert. And any good expert knew it was important to taste her concoction to see that it was dry enough. No one would notice if a bottle of gin occasionally went missing.

Whether she read the articles or not, Alison could not have missed the "nature versus nurture" discussions. Our older brother and I were dark and looked like Mother. Alison was light with blonde hair; she had a double chin and little pushed-in nose. She didn't look like anyone in our family.

Mother sometimes introduced us as her adopted daughters. We were polite enough not to embarrass her on the spot. Perhaps she introduced us like that to create distance or to show she couldn't be responsible for Alison being a lesbian or her older daughter being quiet and shy. She couldn't be the cause of her children's defects. We were adopted, and she had done the best she could with what she had to work with.

At sixteen Alison got her license, a car (I didn't get a car until I was twenty-one), and access to alcohol. Life doesn't get any better for a teenager. Alley had a great sense of humor; she was fun to be with and always had lots of friends. Having a car and access to alcohol made it that much more fun. What does a sixteen-year-old know about moderation? Nothing. She was drinking before school, during school in a gully next to the building, and after school. By the time she was a senior, Alison was an alcoholic. Her grades were good enough to get her into college, so no one noticed.

After she failed out of college and was working at the animal hospital, Alison rented an apartment with her partner, supported herself, and looked as if she were successful. She got involved with photography, developing black-and-white film. She was good at it. But when that relationship ended, so did her interest in developing film, although she continued to take pictures. She got a different apartment with her new partner and got involved with tropical fish (both freshwater and saltwater) and parrots. When that relationship ended, the fish and the birds disappeared.

Sometimes it must have been hard for Alley to have me as a sister. I finished college, and she flunked out after one semester. I finished graduate school and got a job as a middle-school guidance counselor while Alley's life was ravaged by alcohol and pills.

It isn't as if I am smarter than Alison. She had better grades in high school and was accepted to the University of Vermont. I struggled through high school, and my grades were not good enough for admission to UVM. She liked to play a game in which she would call me, always late at night, and ask me a trivia question.

"What president said ..." she would begin.

I would blurt out the first president who popped into my head and say, "Millard Fillmore."

Alley would quickly make a beeping sound and say, "Wrong. You're pretty dumb for someone with a college degree."

"Yep, I guess I am," I told her. "You are smarter than me."

It's true: my younger sister is smarter than I am. But then again, I didn't have all day to watch game shows.

"Just because you have all those degrees doesn't mean you are smarter than me, you know." Her voice would be defensive and sad. I'd hear the ice clinking around in the glass, and she'd take a sip.

"Alley, you're right. I just liked school," I'd confess.

"Travel can be just as much of an education. I learned more on my trip to Africa than you did from graduate school." She'd take another sip, and I knew we would not be having this conversation if she were sober.

It would be the middle of the night for me, and I had to get up in the morning and go to work. "I think travel is very important, too," I would agree. And I did agree with her—travel *is* important.

"We should go to Africa," she'd suggest.

"That would be fun." I was too tired to keep up my end of the fight. Besides, this was a conversation we had had many times at that hour of the night. I knew how it was going to go and how it would end.

"I have been there, but you haven't." My sister was baiting me, but I didn't bite. "You really are dumb for a college graduate. You know that?"

"Yeah, I know that," I agreed.

"I'm smarter than you."

"Yes, Alley, you are smarter than I am."

"You think you are so fucking smart." She is yelling now, upset that I have not given her a reason to fight. I decide not to say anything. "Linny, why did she do that?" I hear more ice clinking and soft cries. "Why did she have to say those things? Why didn't she love me?"

I knew she was talking about our mother, and I knew that "those things" referred to Mother's comments that started with, "Why can't you make yourself prettier?" or "You should …" followed by any number of things. As hurtful as these remarks were, the most painful for Alison was being ignored. It was like living in an airless world.

When Mother wasn't ignoring Alley, she was dropping in at the animal hospital where Alley worked and acting very motherly. The employees at the animal hospital called her the Dragon Lady. She would enter the building and walk around as if she were inspecting it for cleanliness, asking lots of questions. Everyone was too polite to ask her to leave.

"Alley, she couldn't love anyone because she was mentally ill," I said softly and listened to her cry. I knew how this was going to end. "Alley, I know it doesn't help, but she never got over the loss of her own children." Alison said nothing, and I continued.

"She was afraid of losing us like she had lost her two biological children."

After Mother died, I told our mother's older sister, Betty, that Mother had told us that Betty and my uncle didn't like us because we were adopted. "I wish I had known," she said tearfully. "It wasn't true. Your grandmother loved you all. We all loved you. Your mother was crazy." My aunt Betty spat out, "I mean, she needed therapy."

"Had she always been crazy?" I asked my mother's older sister. "I mean, was she a normal little girl?"

"No … she wasn't crazy back then. She was just my sweet baby sister," Betty said, her face softening as she retrieved images of the younger sister in her memory. My aunt looked back at me and continued. "It wasn't until after the babies died—after Tommy was born and we were told he would never leave the hospital. Your mother took Heidi and a nurse and went to Vermont." I had not heard this story before.

"I went to the hospital every day to see that baby boy," she continued. "I made all the decisions about his care, and I held him. Your mother stayed away in Vermont. She never held him. Finally, I called her and told her if she wanted to see him, to come back now."

"Did she return to Massachusetts to see him?"

"Yes, she returned to see him before he died. Then, after Heidi died, your mother was never the same. She got mean. She would get so angry and scream at our mother and say terrible things." Betty stopped talking, and I didn't know what to say, so I just sat quietly in her living room. "Linny, I am so sorry." Betty had always been my funny aunt. She was the one with the sense of humor, the one telling jokes. Now she just looked sad.

"Alley, it wasn't that you were unlovable," I told Alison on the phone later, "or you didn't deserve to be loved. Mother just couldn't love another child." At this point in the conversation, she would be sobbing and unable to talk. I'd wish I could beam myself to Kanab and put my arms around her. I'd wait, hear the ice again, and wait some more.

"It really wasn't so bad," Alison would finally manage. "Our life wasn't so bad. We got to ski and play tennis. Linny, how about we sell both our houses and buy another one together?"

"Where would you like to live?" I ask her.

"Somewhere in the mountains. I love you."

"I love you too, Alley."

"Night."

"Night."

It was always difficult to go back to sleep after these late-night calls. She was in so much pain. I'd put the phone down and roll over, knowing I would not be able to go back to sleep for a while.

They say timing is everything. I don't know about that. But I think for Alison, my five-year head start made the difference. I was adopted into a family with two parents and an older brother. My father was working full time. We all lived together. My grandparents visited us occasionally on holidays, and my grandmother was in her cottage, five miles away, all summer. I went to a nursery school that Mother drove me to and picked me up from. And on my birthdays, I had big birthday parties in the dining room with my friends and lots of presents. My birthday is in December, and Mother always made a huge deal of it so I wouldn't feel I was cheated because it was so close to Christmas.

Alison arrived in the summer before I started first grade. It wasn't long after that that our father lost his full-time job. He was getting up early, spending more time "working" in his tool shed, and falling asleep by noon. About the same time, Mother fell in love with the man who was to be her second husband. Years later, Mother would tell me her marriage to our father ended the day their daughter Heidi died.

When it was time for Alley to go to nursery school, she walked there all by herself. I was home sick one chilly spring day when Alison walked home; we called it mud season in Vermont. She came in the house in her red snowsuit, her face and hands covered with mud.

"What happened?" I asked her. Alison told me the standard poodle that lived in the house by the nursery school followed her home each day, knocked her over, and climbed on top of her.

When Mother got home, I told her what had happened to Alison. She already knew. Mother had known this was happening and had done nothing to protect her four-year-old daughter from a dog twice her size. I called my friend, the son of the owner, to ask him to tell his mother to keep the dog inside.

Lines divided Mother's life into distinct parts, like different chapters. There was her life growing up, the youngest child of three daughters, with her parents and sisters; her marriage to our father; her marriage to Douglas; and her third marriage. Then there was her life with her natural children and her life with her adopted children. Even our chapter was divided between Bobby, me, and Alison.

Why not me instead of Alison? The most important difference for me was my warm and cozy grandmother, Dede. She lived in Massachusetts, but her real home was the cottage her mother had built on Thompson's Point on Lake Champlain.

I was old enough to spend nights with her, sleeping on the second-floor porch next to her. The smell of hot oatmeal with brown sugar and coffee cooked over the wood fire in the kitchen stove would greet me in the morning. I can still hear the creaking floorboards and the slamming of the screen door.

We spent our days playing canasta and Scrabble and watching *Guiding Light*, a popular soap on television. When I was not playing with Dede, I walked in the woods looking at the trillium and gathering twigs to burn in the kitchen stove. The sun would then rise over the tree-covered hill and burn off the early morning dew. I stayed with my grandmother for those early summer weeks between school letting out and when my aunt Betty arrived at my grandmother's cottage from Massachusetts with her three sons. My grandmother would want me to stay, but Mother would insist that I had to come home, because her sister and three nephews had arrived. But for those weeks, I knew I was loved and the most important person in my grandmother's life.

By the time Alison was the same age I had been when I first stayed in my grandmother's care, Dede was too old. I was now old enough to be of help. I had my driver's license and could drive my grandmother to the store. My dear grandmother died of a heart attack when she was eighty and I was eighteen. Alison was only thirteen.

Alison didn't have those wonderful summer days with our grandmother. She didn't experience being wrapped up in line-dried towels and watching a thunderstorm crossing Lake Champlain from the safety of a living room with a fire in the stone fireplace. Alison didn't get to sleep next to her, taking in the smell of her violet perfume and the sound of the lapping waves against the rock face below. No one cut the crusts off her sandwiches and made her butterscotch pudding served in little flower dishes.

One day my mother walked into the living room where I was sitting on the couch, reading a book with Dede. Mother screamed at me. The attack was sudden and unexpected, and I couldn't breathe. My whole body just froze, and I couldn't hear the words, only the hatred. Her screams seemed to go on for hours, and the encounter ended with her abruptly turning, leaving the house, and driving away. My grandmother and I sat there in total silence, not daring to say a word.

My grandmother finally spoke. "Your mother loves you."

How could she say that or even think it? It sure didn't feel like love.

I learned that day that I was not the only one afraid of my mother. I realized that if her own mother could not protect me from her, no one could. I also learned that my grandmother knew there was something wrong with her youngest daughter. Dede would say, "Just keep to the right, and do the best you can."

If Alison was not home with me or our father, she was at any number of homes in the area. Mother was in love with a man twenty-five years older than her. He was too old to have young children running around his well-ordered house. Our presence in his house turned out to be more of an issue for her than it was for him. So, consequently, Alison was dropped off at other homes. Some had children her age, and some had no children living there at all. When she got older, Alison would just walk across the road and stay with the four kids who lived there.

I should have taken her back to Vermont two years ago. The day I left the Hopi reservation, I should have rented a truck and hired some big guys to load up all her stuff and taken her back home

The summer after I left the reservation, Alison came to visit me. My friend Patty and I drove to Boston and picked her up at Logan Airport. My daughter arrived from London a half hour before Alley's plane. When my sister walked down the concourse, our collective breaths were taken away. She was shockingly thin.

My daughter looked at me with a shocked expression and whispered, "Holy shit, what happened to her?"

Alley stayed with me for about ten days. She cleaned out my closet, tossing out clothes I had not worn recently, rearranged furniture with the help of my son, and re-hung pictures on the walls. When she was done, my house looked as if it should be featured in *Good Housekeeping* magazine. We sat on my deck and talked about how beautiful Mount Mansfield looked. Everything was lush and green. The weather was warm with a slight breeze. If only she could move her house to Vermont, she said.

We talked more about sharing a house.

"How about a ski chalet?" she suggested. That sounded good to me. We spent the days grilling and talking about Mother and Douglas, our brother whom we didn't see, and where we should live. I didn't bring up the topic of her drinking, and she knew better than to smoke in my house. And then she returned to Kanab and her little stucco house.

There is no rewind button. Some things we just don't get to do over. We have to do it right the first time. If we could rewind, would we take life so seriously? Would we say regrettable things to our friends and family and then just rewind and carry on as if nothing had been said? Would we smoke and drink ourselves into bad health and then just wipe our lungs and liver clean and start over?

"You think you are so great. You think you are better than me!" Alison would yell, as if she were accusing me of robbing a bank or murdering someone. I didn't think I was great. I thought I was terrible. Just like Alison and Bob, I thought I was unlovable. How did I escape alcoholism? Did I escape? God knows there was always an opportunity right at home to drink.

I know my brother and sister sometimes resented me. On paper—on diploma, actually—I looked good. But my accomplishments had nothing to do with being smart. I was not a good athlete like Bob, and I was not funny and outgoing like Alison. In high school, I was entirely forgettable. I was not a great basketball player and didn't have a lot of friends. I had a few really good friends. My claim to fame was being Bobby and Alison's sister.

My addiction was going to school. I couldn't wait for the first day, to get the new syllabus. I couldn't wait to get back to my deck at home, where I carefully labeled my new binders and organized my day planner. I only really looked forward to snow and the opening of ski season.

On the first day of school, I always enjoyed that my life, at least for the next several months, was laid out in front of me. I found comfort in the predictability of school. I knew how to be a student—not that I got great grades, but it was a role I knew. Here were few surprises. I could avoid the professors who reminded me of my father and seek out the ones who offered me a new view of the world.

After two years at a junior college, I found myself again in a state of anxiety. What was I going to do now? I found a job in a hotel and transferred to another college. My anxiety abated, at least for the next two years. During the day, I studied psychology and sought to make sense of the Vietnam War.

Skiing was the only time I was free of anxiety. I loved the silence that was only broken by the click-click-click of the cable passing through the towers on the ride up on the lift. I would push myself off at the top and carve slow turns in the new snow. The skis were a part of me. I controlled them as easily as my arms and legs. I knew without looking back how my tracks would look in the new snow.

When Mother's cancer returned, she got meaner—not just to us, but to Betty as well. She was mad that her older sister, who drank and smoked, was going to live. She was mad at her three children, because we were going to live and she was going to die. She refused to allow her sister to visit her. Betty would call her every day, but Mother would not even talk to her on the phone. Mother frequently talked to me about changing her will to exclude whatever child she was mad at that day. She was mad at us for living. If she could, she would probably have taken me with her, just so she wouldn't have to go alone. It was unfair; life had asked too much of her. There were unmarried girls having healthy, unwanted babies while her wanted children had died. We were the second string, or maybe the third. We had been sent in only when all else was lost. We didn't really count and would have been dropped from the team and forgotten if the real children could be resurrected.

It was toward the end of Mother's illness that the three of us finally got together. It was then that we expressed our lack of confidence and shared stories of failed relationships. Our mother, the one person who should love us, was still playing each of us against the other from her deathbed.

A couple of days before she died, Mother said again that she wanted to change her will so the money was in trust for Alison and Bob. It would mean that every time they wanted money, the two of them would have to come to me. She could die knowing the two of them would hate me for the rest of their lives.

"You can't control us from the grave, so give it up," I told her. She didn't ask again.

When my son was two and having his second hip surgery, my brother, Bob, came in with balloons that he tied to Pablo's bed and waited with me for him to wake up. Bob left as Alley arrived, and in those few seconds my brother and sister passed in the hall, the phone rang. There was no hello, no "How is Pablo? How are you holding up?" My mother did not say any of those loving things. Instead she said, "Bob said that you are lower than a pile of shit, and if he never saw you again, it would be too soon." I said thanks and hung up.

I sat back down and looked from my sister to my son. Alison said to let it go, forget about it, but I couldn't, no matter what I said to myself, telling myself Mother was crazy. Bob had just been there. He had brought Pablo balloons; he had sat right there, where Alison was now sitting, for over an hour; and he had been nice to me.

I had never gone around Mother before, but later that same night, I called my brother and asked if he had said those words to Mother.

"If I have something to say about you, I will say it to you," he said. Two days later, I asked Mother why she had thought she needed to tell me Bob's opinion of me when my son was waking up from surgery.

"Because you needed to know," she defended herself.

"Would your mother have called you when Heidi was having her heart operation and said Betty thought you were lower than shit?" I asked her.

"No, my mother would never say something so mean."

"Then why did you say something so mean?" I asked her. She was silent. I stood up, walked out of her kitchen, and went home to my children.

Alison and I did work hard to overcome the distrust, but we did not escape Mother's damage. We would remind one another she couldn't divide and conquer anymore, but the lingering voice remained to tell us that love is conditional.

Not only was Mother's love conditional on us behaving, but we needed to be grateful as well. On a night my parents gave a dinner party, I passed out cheese and crackers. When the company sat down to eat, I quickly gathered up the used glasses and ashtrays. When the guests returned to the living room for coffee and dessert, I cleared away the dinner dishes. While I fed the plates into the dishwasher, a friend of my mother's came into the kitchen. She told me what a good job I was doing.

"You must feel very grateful to be living in such a nice house," she said.

I don't remember what she said next. I remember thinking that if I wasn't grateful and helpful, they would give me away. Was I supposed to feel grateful? Why was this friend of my mother saying this to me? Did my childhood friends Linda and Lydia and Ronda feel grateful to have parents and their nice houses? I don't think I ever really understood, but we learned not to be a bother or inconvenient.

In the process of cleaning out Mother's file drawer, I found three folders marked "Bob," "Linda," and "Alison." Inside each were newspaper clippings. In the one labeled with my name were my college graduation announcements from the local newspaper. In the ones for Bob and Alison were newspaper clippings with their names in the "Day In Court" column for their DUIs. I put them all in the shedder.

So she had known I had graduated with my master's degree. I was the only one of her children to finish college. I had wanted her to be proud of me. I wasn't drinking and doing drugs and wrecking cars. I had a full-time professional job. She wasn't hiring a lawyer to fix my DUIs, but I wasn't getting her attention for playing by the rules, either. It didn't matter how successful I was; she would always find a reason to criticize.

After Mother had been dead for fifteen years, Alison was still cleaning her house and trying to lose her double chin. It was Mother's love she had to win, or die trying. All those years, the three of us had been so busy protecting ourselves or doing something to get Mother's attention when we could have been friends.

During my daughter's senior year in high school, my daughter and I flew to Seattle, Washington, to look at colleges. I talked Alley into joining us. She arrived first. I found her in the hotel bar, sitting on a bar stool, chatting with a female bartender. I stood at a distance, just watching her, before I let her know I had arrived. In all these years, we had never gone to a bar together. I was seeing an Alison I didn't know. She spoke fluent barese; it was like her first language. I parked myself on the stool next to her as she popped some peanuts into her mouth. She offered no greeting, no "How was your flight?" or "Where is Vida?" Alison just asked if I wanted a drink, knowing I didn't drink.

My introduction to bars had come at an early age. Starting at sixteen, I was sent out to pick up my father. He would go into a bar, alone or with a friend, and get drunk. At that point, the bartender would call and ask that someone come and get him. They had no trouble taking his money, but they found his intoxication too difficult to handle.

One night, after getting the summons to come and fetch him, I found my father and a friend, both drunk, singing with a drunken piano player. All three were singing, "Sam, You Made the Pants Too Long." I sat through a couple of verses, trying to work out what I was going to do. I got them both into the backseat of the station wagon. They were like bookends with no books to hold up—just each other.

I took the friend home first. Opening the back door of the car, I pulled him out onto the driveway. I honked the horn for someone to come get him and left him there. It was summer, and I knew neither of them would freeze to death. Then I went home, parked the car, got out, and walked into the house.

Our father wasn't a mean or bad person. When he wasn't passed out, he was a sweet guy. He had been born nine years after his sister. His father had been a patent lawyer and his older brother a successful businessman. Johnny, as my father was called, grew up spoiled by his mother. His best friend was engaged to my mother's older sister, Betty, so Johnny just followed him over to his girlfriend's house.

That is how our mother met him. He was nine years older, was handsome in his army uniform, and had gone to college. He was from a good family, and her parents liked him. No one knew that he already had a drinking problem. My mother did not get the older, mature man she thought she was getting.

When I was a little girl, I loved my father. "Do you know how much I love you?" he would ask me.

"Yes, you tell me all the time," I would answer. But later, I didn't like him. After his heart attack and stroke, sadness cloaked him and I felt a responsibility to do something. Every Tuesday night for the last several months of his life, I took him out for dinner. I ate, and he had two double martinis. He lived in a motel across from the restaurant, so I could just take him home and pour him into his bed.

On a Tuesday night, there was an ice storm, and I couldn't make it. My father went across the street anyway to have his usual martinis. Crossing the street to his motel, he was struck by a car. He died a month later in the hospital. Alison and I cleaned out his motel room. One entire wall was lined with empty liquor bottles. The bedding was spotted with cigarette burns from his four-pack-a-day habit. We put everything into the Dumpster except the watch his father had given him. Alison strapped it on her wrist and wore it until it stopped running.

Chapter Eleven: Day Six

I listen to Alison suck in air like a trout on the bottom of a canoe. This would be the point where I would be begging Alley to hurry up and get the hook out and toss the poor fish back in High Pond, the stocked pond on our stepfather's farm. My chest hurts with the effort to breathe for her. I want to help. I want to breathe for her. I can't. I am scared. I don't know how to help my sister. It is early; the sun is not yet up. There is only the light from the night light in the bathroom.

"Linny!" my sister calls from the trough, the low point, between the waves. There is nothing I can do. I can only watch from the deck of her bed. She is so frightened.

"You shouldn't have leaned so far out over the railing," I want to yell down at her. I want to rescue her, lower a lifeboat, turn the ship around, toss in a life ring, and jump in after her, and I want to drown her myself for being so goddamn stupid. *How could she do this to herself? Who the hell does she think she is for putting me though this? What gives her the right to leave me here all alone?*

"Linny?" she pleads with me to save her. I can see it in her eyes. They are so big and hold mine, and I can't look away.

I get up on my knees, slide myself under her, and sit back on my feet. Every bone in her body rattles against me with each intake of air and each exhale. I am frightened she will break in my arms. The change in position seems to be helping, but not enough. Leaning ever so slightly, I pull over extra pillows and wedge them in between us to elevate her a little more.

"Alley, you are going to be okay. I've got you," I tell her over and over. I continue giving her encouragement to keep fighting and to keep breathing. *Please don't die*, I beg her silently. *All these years growing up, when I thought you needed me, it was me needing you. I don't want you to die. How do I let go of everything we have shared?* I will her to read my thoughts so I don't have to say them out loud. Saying them out loud would be admitting that my sister might die.

The sun is now beginning to rise, and I can just make out the outline of the tree outside her window.

"Linny," she says through the liquid in her throat. "Linny."

She trusts me to take care of her, as if we are going to wake up from this nightmare or the director will yell "cut" and the waves will stop—as if the deck I am standing on is not attached to a ship being tossed about in the ocean. I am kneeling on Alison's king-sized bed, and she is filling with fluids not from the ocean, but from inside her body.

The hospice woman had said to call if Alison needed anything or if I needed anything. She reminded me that there was a no-resuscitation order—that when Alison stopped breathing, there would be no calls to the rescue squad. It sounded right at the time. *Yes*, I said. *I understand*, I said. There was to be no keeping her alive by heroic measures. It would be cruel and mean to keep my sister alive; I know it would just prolong her suffering. The no-resuscitation order is what Alison wants and what I believe to be right.

As she struggles to inhale air into her oxygen-starved body, Alison's eyes widen with fear and her inability to understand what is happening to her. Fighting to get to the surface, she says, "Linny, help."

Wrapping my arms around my baby sister, holding her frail frame to me, I talk to her softly, telling her she is going to be fine.

How do I do this? I want to do this right. I have promised Alley many times that I will always take care of her. I want to keep my promise. I want to take care of her for as long as she needs me.

"Alley, honey, I am going to lower you just a little, so I can reach the phone." My legs refuse to move. I can't unfold them or get out from under Alley without hurting her. Very carefully, I reach out with the arm not holding Alison and stretch until I feel the receiver. I pull the whole thing onto the bed and dial the number the hospice nurses gave me.

"Hello?" answers a female voice on the second ring. It is just before six in the morning, and she sounds as if she is wide awake.

"This is Linda, Alison Booth's sister. I need help."

"What is going on, Linda?"

"She can't breathe. Please come … now," I beg. I want to cry and say I am so scared and don't want to be alone. I want to confess I can't do this by myself. But I can't. I can't admit I can't handle it. I have always been the one my family relied on. I sat with my father as he lay in a coma, and on my stepfather's bed when he died, and with my mother until moments before she died, and now with Alison.

"We will be right there," I hear the voice say, and then the line goes dead.

"Okay, Alley," I say, projecting total confidence that everything will be okay, "the nurse is on her way, and you are going to be fine." My little sister is dying. It is not going to be fine. I know Alley can't be fixed. She isn't going to have a fast recovery that will allow the two of us to drive up to Bryce Canyon to take photos.

I called the nurse for myself, to help me. I am not ready to lose my sister. I am not ready to be alone in the world. I want more time with her. I need time to talk and time to … I am just not ready to let go. Maybe she will keep eating two or three yogurts and a couple of fruit smoothies, and then we can work up to toast.

I hear the front door open, and seconds later, the hospice worker and the nurse walk into Alley's bedroom.

The nurse goes right to Alison. "Alison, can you hear me?" she asks.

"Yes," says Alison, struggling to push the words through the ocean of phlegm.

"I am going to reach into your mouth," she says at the same time she inserts her crooked finger past Alley's lips and pulls out a wad of slime that has accumulated in the back of Alison's throat.

The tears I have managed to delay now stream soundlessly down my cheeks. The nurse supports Alison's body, allowing me to pull my legs out from under her.

"This is normal," the hospice worker says, placing a comforting hand on my back.

"I know," I cry. I do know. I know this is how my sister will die. Death is normal. I can do nothing. I have no control. But first, I want Alley to know how much I love her.

"She was so frightened," I tell the worker through the tears. "She was so scared."

"I think she would be more comfortable in a hospital bed," suggests the nurse.

"I'll call." The hospice worker walks from the room with her cell phone in her hand.

"She will be more comfortable now," the nurse says sympathetically. She turns from Alley to look at me. "When did you last give her morphine?"

"Ah ..." I try to remember, but I can't. "I'll check," I say, walking from the room to the breakfast bar, where I have been keeping the drugs and chart.

I return with everything and hand the drug chart to the nurse. She glances at it quickly and then, after pulling on surgical gloves, rubs the anti-anxiety cream on Alley's thin arms. "This will help your sister. She will be calmer." She gives Alison more morphine before she pulls off the gloves and adjusts pillows under and around Alison. Then she very carefully arranges my sister's arms and legs, as if Alison is a large Raggedy Ann doll.

She is gentle with my sister. Alison deserves to have people treat her gently and with love. The wrecked cars and drunken rants don't matter now. All that matters is that I love her and that she knows.

"You can give her a little more morphine; she will be more comfortable, less agitated."

"They are bringing the bed right now," says the hospice worker as she reenters Alley's bedroom.

"Good," responds the nurse. "We can wait and move her." The three of us stand around Alison's bed. The two of them talk in low voices, and we wait. I feel empty, vacant, and drained. I look at Alison; her eyes are closed, and she looks peaceful.

The hospice worker moves closer to me. "There is a no-resuscitation order for your sister," she reminds me.

"Yes, I know," I answer her. I don't understand why she is saying this to me again. Does she not want me to call her for help? Are they really busy with other patients?

"This is normal," she says, trying to be reassuring.

"I know," I say again. I do know this is normal, but it is not normal for me to watch my younger sister die.

"I know," I repeat just above a whisper. "Yes, it is just … I couldn't …"

Just then the hospital bed arrives, and a woman and man carry the parts in and assemble them at the foot of Alison's bed.

"Alley," I say, leaning over my sister's head and calling her to the surface of the grim reality that is her life. "Alley, we are going to move you to the hospital bed."

She opens her eyes wide and looks around, trying to understand why all these people are in her room.

"No! You will drop me. Please!" She begins to cry.

"Alley, we won't drop you, I promise. We won't drop you."

The nurse and the hospice worker don't wait for Alison to be soothed. They roll up the sides of the blanket and slide her closer to the edge of the bed. They have done this before.

"No!" cries Alison is total terror. "Stop! Please, no!"

The five of us lift Alley along with her bedding onto the narrower hospital bed, and again the nurse takes great care to smooth the sheets after she arranges Alley's legs. She untangles the blankets, folds over the top, and places Alley's bruised hands on top of her belly. Alison is exhausted, her eyes are closed, and she is breathing easier. The woman and the man who brought the bed leave, taking the walker and wheelchair they brought over a week ago. The hospice administrator and the nurse leave as well. I am alone with Alley again.

I don't know where to put myself or what to do. I have cleaned everything there is to clean, but I haven't watered Alley's garden. I open the door to the outside and look at the garden my sister has lovingly taken care of and nurtured since she bought the house eight years ago. The wind chimes sound discordant. Climbing the steps, I walk the path around the tree that serves as the centerpiece of her backyard; I end up at the top of the steps and sit down. With my elbows propped on my knees, my head falls into my open hands. I am feeling everything and feeling nothing. There must be something I should be doing, but I don't know what it is. Lowering my hands to my knees, I push myself up and walk back inside. I take my place next to the mechanical hospital bed, lean heavily on the top rail, and stare at Alley.

"Alley?" I whisper. I say it a little louder. She doesn't stir.

I want her to open her eyes. I want her to say, "Hi, Linny," but she doesn't hear me. I want to talk to my sister. I don't know what I want to hear. I don't know what she wants to hear. I place a hand on her head. She looks peaceful, serene. I just keep rubbing her head.

When I was here two weeks ago, Alley sank into my lap. She took my hand and placed it on her head and moved it back and forth. I rubbed her head for hours that day.

I untangle her hair by running my finger through the thinning brown strands. I wish I could have really colored her hair. I want so much to take her to Africa and Hong Kong and China. I am so grateful that we got to go to Greece together.

I keep rubbing her head and combing my fingers through her hair. Does she know I am here? Can she feel me touching her? Can she hear my voice as I tell her how much I love her?

I don't know what to do. I don't know how to be. There is nothing I can do except wait for Alley to wake up and ask for yogurt and coffee. Her bed is stripped of sheets and blankets, down to the mattress pad. I think about finding some clean sheets and remaking it but give up the idea and lie down on the left side of the bed—Alley's place. I listen to Alison breathing. It is a steady, unlabored, natural rhythm. She is sleeping. She needs the sleep. She will feel better when she wakes up.

I wake up suddenly. The light has changed. How long have I been asleep? I sit up with my legs hanging off the side of the bed. I walk out to the kitchen and make coffee for myself. I make enough so I can microwave some for Alley later. I pour myself a bowl of Frosted Flakes, add milk, pass the bowl of cereal and mug of black coffee through the opening, and set them on the breakfast bar.

My plan is to perch on a bar stool where I have an unobstructed view down the hall, so I can watch Alley sleeping in the hospital bed. I settle on one stool and stretch out my legs across another. Dax strides toward me and I remember I didn't feed them this morning. I forgot.

"I am so sorry. Come on, Dax, I will get you something to eat," I say. A noise gets my attention. From the top of the kitchen cabinets, Marco Polo stands and stretches like a large Halloween cat. Without warning, he is on the stove top and then lands with a light thud on the floor.

"Okay, okay," I say, begging for forgiveness. They do figure eights between my legs until I get the food into the separate bowls.

"I am sorry." I keep apologizing. Alley would be upset if she knew I hadn't fed Dax and Marco Polo early this morning.

"How is she?" LeAnn asks just above a whisper, walking in the open door. "I saw the bed being moved in." Living directly across the street had made it possible for LeAnn to keep an eye on Alison. When Alison and I talked about her moving back to Vermont, she always said that if LeAnn moved, she would be out of here in a heartbeat.

"They thought she would be more comfortable," I answer, standing up and tossing the empty can into the trash. "Alley had a difficult time breathing during the night."

LeAnn turns, and we both look down the hall. With my cereal and coffee abandoned, we move to opposite sides of Alley's bed. LeAnn rubs her arm affectionately.

"She looks peaceful," she whispers without taking her eyes off her friend. During their years as neighbors, they have shared pet sitting for Alley's two cats and LeAnn's dog and cats. All the animals know about the pet door that leads into Alley house, including Grizzle, LeAnn's rat terrier.

"I remember the first time I met Alison," LeAnn begins slowly. "She was already living here when we moved in. She walked over and introduced herself. It's really nice having her here." Her eyes never leave my sister's face. "She would feed the cats and Grizzle for me when I had to be out of town. And I would feed Dax and Marco when she went to Vermont to see you."

We make small talk, because it is too painful to talk about what we are really thinking about. We withdraw into our own silent thoughts while standing opposite one another with Alison between us. Then, just as silently, we both drift back to the living room. I return to my post on the barstool. LeAnn turns the upholstered chair around and sits down facing me.

"I just want to sit here so I can keep an eye on Alley, just in case she wakes up and wants something." I explain. I pick up my bowl and take a bit of the cereal. It's soggy. I lose interest and put it back down on the bar.

"Linda, how are you doing?" asks LeAnn.

"Okay," I answer. What is there to say? How can I tell her what it feels like to lose a sister?

"When my mother was here visiting, she came over to see Alison. My mother really likes her. They have a special bond. My mother is also adopted."

"Adopted kids tend to find one another. It's funny how that happens," I say offhandedly.

"Alison said you are going to help her find her birth mother. She showed me the letter you sent. I think she was really happy to get that," LeAnn shares.

"Yes, first I read it to her over the phone before putting it in the mail. When I read her the part about how much her mother loved her but just couldn't take care of her because she had a son with chronic health issues, Alley cried."

Alison asked me a couple of years ago to help her find her birth parents. I said I would try but could make no promises. I had found my own birth mother, so Alley thought I could find hers as quickly. I started with the agency in Vermont that had placed her in our family. They would not give me any identifying information but did write a nice letter explaining the circumstances of Alison's birth and why she had been relinquished for adoption. They wrote that Alison's birth mother loved her very much but was unable to take care of a sick child and a newborn. There was nothing about Alley's mother being found unconscious in her car while pregnant.

"Alison said that was enough for her. She said it was enough to know her mother loved her and that she had a brother. She asked me not to look for her."

Before LeAnn could respond, a voice from outside the door facing the garden startles us both: "Hello?"

"Come on in," says LeAnn, turning in her chair to look at Michelle.

"How is she doing?" asks Michelle, craning her neck to look down the hall.

"She's sleeping," I say to the smoothie lady. "She had a really hard night. Had trouble breathing and didn't get much sleep."

"Have you had any sleep?"

"I'm not tired," I tell her.

Michelle drags a rattan chair over from the opposite corner of the living room, where all the shipping boxes had been the day before. LeAnn and Michelle talk about native plants. I have nothing to contribute, and besides, I cannot keep up with the conversation. I keep looking down the hall at Alley.

"I'm going to go home," says LeAnn, standing up. "Call me if you need me." LeAnn walks over to where I am perched on the bar stool and gives me a hug. "I will make you something to eat. You need to eat." LeAnn turns and goes out the front door. I can picture her stepping on to the gravel and walking down to the road, where she will be greeted by her cats and Grizzle.

"I should have brought you a smoothie," Michelle says, giving me a concerned look. "I would make you one now, but Alison doesn't have a blender."

I smile, because earlier, I saw a blender in the cupboard where Alison keeps the cat food. "She has a blender," I tell Michelle.

"She told me she didn't have one. Why would she tell me she didn't have a blender?"

I know why Alison told Michelle she didn't have a blender. "If Al had to get out the blender, clean it after, and put it away, a smoothie wouldn't have been a gift. She wouldn't have had the feeling of being taken care of," I explain.

I watch Michelle's face to see if she understands why Alison lied about not having a blender. My sister is so hungry for mothering that even something as simple as someone making a smoothie is a special gift. It is more than a gift. It would have felt to Alison as if she were a little girl again, but with a mother who loved her. This is what mommies do; they make their children smoothies.

"I wish I had met her earlier," Michelle says. "I think I could have made a difference."

"I think you could have too," I tell her. I don't tell her that many people have thought they could make a difference. Sometimes love and friendship isn't enough.

"Alison was paying me to work in her garden—you know, some weeding and keeping things watered. Sometimes we would sit and talk. She talked about her sister in Vermont a lot. She also told me how much fun she had with you in Greece. She really loves you. I never charged her for the time we sat and chatted," she quickly informs me, afraid I will think she took advantage of Alison.

"Michelle, I need to lie down for a minute." Suddenly I feel light-headed and a little shaky. Michelle follows me down the hall to Alison's bedroom.

"Oh, baby girl, what have you done to yourself?" the best smoothie lady in the world asks my sleeping sister. She stands over her for a few minutes as if perhaps she is expecting an answer.

After a few minutes of standing next to the railing, watching Alley sleep, Michelle lies down on the bed next to me.

After a few minutes of silence, Michelle says, "Alison always liked it when I brought Asher over to visit." She looks up at the ceiling fan. "Asher is my rescue greyhound." We lie there is silence. "I'll run home and get her. Alison will like seeing her."

"Okay," I respond. I don't know if I should encourage or discourage the dog's visit. I don't have the brain cells to form an opinion one way or the other.

I want to talk to Alison. I want to say I'm sorry that I couldn't protect her from Mother and that I'm sorry I didn't do something the first time she got caught drinking back in the high school. *Alley, what could I have done? What did you want me to do?* I ask her inside my head.

"You were always so angry," I say out loud.

I want to ask her if she had a good time in Greece. I want to ask her why she sat and read a book and drank wine all day instead of exploring. Was any of the trip fun? She yelled at me if I suggested a walk or a bus ride or offered her some good local fruit. The only time she got excited was the ferry trip back to Athens. She stood on the top deck, taking pictures of the Aegean islands.

Asher, with his sleek brindle greyhound body, lands on the bed next to me. "Asher, you get down," commands Michelle.

"It's okay," I tell her. But he jumps down anyway with a little yelp. Alison jerks awake, startled, and opens her eyes. Michelle goes to her bedside and leans on the rail.

"I brought Asher over to see you," she tells Alison.

Alison doesn't say a word. I sit up and go to Alison.

"You want a smoothie?" asks Michelle. If anything can get Alison's interest, it will be a smoothie. "I can run home and make one," offers Michelle. She seems to understand that a smoothie is love. Alison doesn't answer.

"It's five o'clock," says Michelle in an "oh darn" voice. "I have to go feed my mother. My mother has to have her dinner at five. I'll come back and bring you a strawberry smoothie. Bye, Alison. I will see you later."

"Later," Alley whispers through a new buildup of phlegm.

I watch Michelle and Asher walk together down the hall and out of sight. "Alley, you want anything, coffee?" I ask her.

"No," she struggles to say through the fluid in her throat. All this time she has been asleep, fluid has been filling up again. I crank up the head of the bed a little, but it doesn't seem to make her breathing easier, so I raise it a little more. Her lungs and throat are filling so fast—much faster than this morning. My sister's eyes go big with fear. She has already been through this once. I can have the nurse come back and clear her throat. They would not be resuscitating Alley, just clearing out the phlegm.

I move from her bedside to make the call. I tell them I need them.

"Alley, the nurse is on her way over. You are going to be okay," I quickly reassure her. "Alley?" I start to ask if she needs anything but then stop myself.

"Linny, fix it," Alison says, forcing the words through the liquid. The sound is frightening, and her eyes reflect the terror. She wants me to fix what she has done to herself, to make it all better, to make it go away. She doesn't take her eyes from my face. She wants me to clear the fluid making its way up to drown her. Her body is betraying her. She weighs only sixty-three pounds. If only she had agreed to go to the nursing home. I wouldn't have left. I would have stayed right here in Kanab, Utah, until she was well enough to go back to Vermont. But she wanted to come home—not to die, but to make sure her house was perfect. I don't know how to remove the liquid from her throat.

"Alley, I can't," I say. "You have gone too far this time." I tell her this because I don't know what else to do or say.

Her eyes go wider. She doesn't want to die. *What a stupid thing to say—I have to do better than that.* It's not like I know the right thing to say. This is not a dress rehearsal; we don't get to keep doing it over until we get it right. We don't get to treat our bodies badly or say hurtful things to people and then have it erased and do it over. This isn't the movie *Groundhog Day*, in which Bill Murray wakes up to the same day, day after day, until he gets it right.

I understand my sister's desire to go back to her age of innocence and grow up again as my third child. I have never felt so helpless. I don't know how to save her. I didn't know what to do when we were children. I have done the only thing I know to do, and that is to call the nurse. I have to do better than to tell her she has gone too far this time.

"Honey," I say to Alley in a calm and confident voice. I lean in close and she focuses on me. "Alley, I will make a deal with you." I see relief in her eyes. She thinks at long as I don't let go, she will survive what she has done to herself. "Here's the deal," I say to let her know the deal is on its way. She nods to indicate she is listening. She trusts. She believes I can save her. She is betting her life on it.

"Today," I say to her slowly to lessen her anxiety, "today is my day to be in charge. Okay?" Her eyes are totally fixed on me. "Alley, I am in charge today, and I will take care of everything. And I promise you that today everything is going to be fine, because I am in charge." Alley nods again, and I see trust and relief in her face. "Now listen," I say, as if this is the really important part, "because there is a condition. Here is the deal part." She nods again, willing to make any deal. "The deal is that tomorrow, you have to be in charge."

"Deal." My baby sister pushes the word through a tidal wave in her throat. Her expression is peaceful; she is confident that I can fix whatever is going on. I know she loves me, and she knows how much I love her.

The hospice worker and nurse burst into the room, and the nurse hurries to Alison's side, lowering the bed. At the same time, the nurse rolls Alley toward her and pulls the liquid from her mouth. When my sister's windpipe is clear, the nurse very gently rolls Alley onto her back.

I look at my sister's face, into her eyes. I don't see relief or trust. The trust she just bestowed on me seconds ago for my ability to take care of any scrape she has gotten herself into is gone. I see nothing. Her eyes are fixed, and she isn't seeing me.

I thought I had months or at least several weeks, to hold her close and for her to tell me how good the yogurt is. She can't be dying—not today. I'm not ready. I promised her that everything would be fine today, because I am in charge today. She believed me.

I touch her arm and then her head. I want to jump into whatever line she is in and get ahead of her. I want to hurry up and go to wherever she is going, so I am there to greet her. I want to make sure she will be okay. I want to be sure she will be safe. I want to protect her from Mother. *Oh, please be kind to her*, I plead. *I promised her today I would be in charge and that she would be fine today. I promised her. Oh, God—where's my sister?*

177

"It won't be long now," whispers the nurse, holding a stethoscope to her chest. "Do you want to lie down with her?" she asks. "We can lower the rail."

I shake my head no. I can't move. I can't breathe. I can't speak. Her eyes are open. I look into them, and there is nothing: no recognition, no peace, and no fear. I hold her hand with one of mine and rub her head with the other, as I have for the past five days.

As if she is handling fine china, the nurse pulls the sheet aside and straightens Alison's legs, pulls down the legs of the warm-up pants, and gently tucks my sister in. Alison is again the precious little curly-haired baby my grandmother held the day Alison was carried into the house by our mother. The hospice worker moves close to me and with a hand on my back says, "You can talk to her; she will hear you."

I can say nothing. I say it inside my head and, using our hands like a telephone cable, I send all my love, my need for her, my fear, and my sadness. I send all this through my fingers. I know she will understand.

"Linda, we can lower the railing," the hospice worker says, and she does so. I can feel the tears sliding down my face and do nothing to stop them.

"It is over," the nurse says gently.

I nod. "I have to get LeAnn," I tell them. My voice is mechanical and flat. I walk out the door and across the street.

LeAnn opens the door. "Alley just died." I don't really need to tell her; she knows. LeAnn begins to cry. I turn, and she follows me as we walk back across the street together. She goes to Alison's side, and I stand at the foot of the hospital bed where Alison lies.

"You want me to call the mortuary?" asks the hospice worker.

I nod.

She leaves the room and returns in what seems like a minute or two with two tall and large men dressed in black suits who look like twins. They introduce themselves and give me time to understand their presence in the room.

"You have asked that she be cremated, is that correct?" one of the brothers asks.

"Yes, my sister wants … wanted to be cremated."

"You understand she will be cremated just as she is?" the same man asks in a low, soft voice.

"Yes," I answer.

After a few minutes, he asks, "Is there anything you want?"

"Want?" I am puzzled.

"Linda," explains the nurse, "Alison will be cremated with what she has on."

I look down from the foot of the bed at my little sister wearing my favorite Hopi T-shirt, my blue warm-up pants, and my watch. "Yes, okay." I tell the nurse.

"Is there anything you want to keep?" I look at the nurse and then realize what she is asking me.

"May I have my watch back?" I say it as if I am asking for permission. I am asking Alison for permission, because I told her she could have it. The nurse takes off the watch and hands it to me.

"What about the rings?" she inquires.

I look down at Alley's fingers resting on top of the blanket. She is wearing two metal rings.

The hospice worker, the nurse, the brothers from the mortuary, and LeAnn all look at me. I am laughing. I look from the nurse to the men in the black suits and to LeAnn.

"She stole them," I tell everyone, looking at each with their puzzled expressions. "The last time I took Alison to the supermarket, she stole them from a display at the cash register. When we got in the car, she said, 'Look what I have!' I said I would go back inside and pay for them. She said not to, that it would take all the fun out of it. I meant to go back later and pay for them, but I forgot. Let's let her keep them."

Good one, Linny, I hear Alley say inside my head, and then she laughs. Alley's laugh is so honest that it makes me smile even as my sadness deepens. I can't believe my sister is dead. The brothers go back down the hall I carpeted three weeks ago to get a gurney. I don't want to watch them remove Alley from her house, so I go outside and sit on the top railroad tie of the three steps leading from her patio up to the natural garden on the upper level.

The nurse sits down next to me. "You and your sister had a very special relationship. I wish I could have known her."

"Yes, we did. We had a special relationship." I wipe my face with both my hands.

The afternoon sun falls lower in the sky, sending a gentle breeze to play over the wind chimes like fingers over black-and-white keys. What has always been noise to me and kept me from sleep is now music.

I twist around and look from one wind chime to the other. They hang in graduated lengths. They play in different keys. There are six of them. What had been irritating to me was music to Alison. And in the music, I hear her laugh.

"Linny, I wish you had been my mother. If you had been my mom, I wouldn't be here," says my little sister.

Chapter Twelve

Alison Chapin Booth from Charlotte, Vermont, passed away June 6, 2008, after a long illness. Alison graduated from Chaplain Valley Union High School and attended the University of Vermont. For over eighteen years, she worked for Dr. Steven Metz at the Shelburne Veterinary Hospital. She is survived by her sister, Linda Booth Burden of Shelburne, and Linda's children, Pablo and Vida Fodor. She is also survived by her brother, Robert Booth of Essex Junction, and his sons, Nicolas and Christopher. For the past eight years, Alison lived in southern Utah, enjoying and photographing the amazing beauty of the Southwest. She touched many lives with her outgoing, generous spirit and unique humor.

We had so much fun in her garden, taking photos and assembling solar fountains. On clear nights, we sat in her hot tub, and Alison pointed out the constellations. I was impressed with her knowledge of the names and relations of each.

I pull a piece of paper from my shorts pocket and sit down hard and exhausted on the top step. Unfolding the paper, I reread the obituary. I wrote it myself, but the reality is still elusive. Being her older sister has been like watching a monster storm gather itself in the distance; you know it is coming, you know it is going to be bad, and you are helpless to prevent the damage. I didn't turn away from the storm that ravaged my sister. I watched as it advanced and threatened to take me with it, too.

I was a kid myself. I could be the "good kid" to my brother's and sister's "bad kid." I thought I could be the perfect kid. But the casting of the good child rotated, not because of anything we did or didn't do, but by some unpredictable, totally random brain function of our mother.

It would have taken an intervention by two cooperative, sober parents to pluck Alison from the path of the approaching storm.

I am sure Alley's death seemed sudden. It wasn't sudden. My sister had been dying for the last thirty-five years. The people in Kanab spoke of weight loss and outrageous behavior. "She was a character, but she had a problem," they'd say. Alley's friends from Vermont will remember the DUIs (tickets for driving under the influence) and say, "I thought she stopped drinking and went out west to work in an animal sanctuary." None of them saw the dark clouds on the horizon, obscured by stern instructions to not discuss family business. "Nothing leaves these four walls," Mother always threatened.

Alison's destiny was sealed the day the adoption agency placed her in our family. The deck was stacked; she was dealt a pair of damaged parents. She was frequently left in our father's care. Even by the time she was five, she had never seen him sober. Dad would be asleep by noon, as he'd been up at four "working" in his tool shed.

Before she entered high school, my little sister already knew how to make a perfect dry martini. Mother was absent, escaping her drunken husband and the isolation and loneliness of staying at home with three small children.

Mother and Dad lived through the deaths of her two biological children, but they didn't survive. Mother defended herself against future heartbreak by keeping her adopted children at a distance. This distance was to blame for the lack of supervision that gave Alison the opportunity to medicate herself with the drug most available.

My sister's obituary should say she was funny, musically talented, a gifted photographer, a hell of a skier and tennis player, an alcoholic, an addict, and loved by her sister. She was not famous. Her death did not make headlines, and no one will be begging for the details of her life and death. The beautiful child who was my sister will not be remembered, except by me, her brother, and a few friends.